*f*rancesco *G*uicciardini

Maxims
and
Reflections
(Ricordi)

TRANSLATED BY
MARIO DOMANDI

INTRODUCTION BY
NICOLAI RUBINSTEIN

University of Pennsylvania Press
Philadelphia

First *Pennsylvania Paperback* edition 1972

Reprinted by arrangement with HARPER & ROW PUBLISHERS

LIBRARY OF CONGRESS CATALOG CARD NUMBER: 64-23752

ISBN: 0-8122-1037-9

MAXIMS
AND
REFLECTIONS
(*Ricordi*)

Contents

Introduction

BY NICOLAI RUBINSTEIN

I

In the history of Renaissance thought, Guicciardini's *Ricordi* occupy a place of singular importance. Few works of the sixteenth century allow us so penetrating an insight into the views and sentiments of its author as these reflexions of the great Italian historian, written down over a period of eighteen years. Like Machiavelli's *Prince*, the *Ricordi* form one of the outstanding documents of a time of crisis and transition; but unlike the *Prince*, they range over a wide field of private as well as public life. In doing so, they reveal the man as well as the political theorist.

* * *

IN JANUARY 1512, Francesco Guicciardini left Florence for the Spanish court as ambassador to the king of Aragon. It was Francesco's first major appointment, and one that was remarkable on account of his youth: "No one could remember at Florence that so young a man had ever been chosen for such an embassy," he writes in his diary.[1] Born in 1483, Franceso, after studying law in Florence, Ferrara, and Padua, had become a successful lawyer in his native city, and had already been elected to minor posts in the republic. As a member of an ancient patrician family, he now followed in the footsteps of his father, grandfather, and great-uncle, who all had held high positions in the government and diplomatic service of Florence. During the fifteenth century, his family had raised their political status

---

[1] "Ricordanze," in Francesco Guicciardini, *Scritti autobiografici e rari*, ed. R. Palmarocchi (Bari, 1936), p. 69.

by supporting the Medici, and Jacopo and Luigi, Francesco's grandfather and great-uncle, had belonged to Lorenzo the Magnificent's inner circle. Francesco's father Piero, although less active in public life, continued to hold office under the new republican regime. Thus when, in October 1511, the Council of Eighty elected Francesco ambassador to Spain, the future may well have seemed mapped out for the young lawyer. Service to the state was in the tradition of the Florentine aristocracy, and this embassy would normally have been the first of many high offices in the republic; but Francesco's career was changed by a sequence of political events. During his absence in Spain, the Spanish and Papal forces advanced on Florence, since 1494 a loyal ally of France, and forced her to recall the Medici, who restored their political supremacy and abolished the republican institutions that had been set up in 1494. In 1513, Lorenzo the Magnificent's son Giovanni became Pope Leo X and placed Florence under Papal control. A side-effect of Florence's new dependency on Rome was that individual Florentines might be appointed to posts in the Papal administration. Guicciardini was one of these. After his return to Florence in 1514, he had been elected a member of the Eight of Ward, and then of the *Signoria*; but soon much wider opportunities opened up for him outside his native city. In 1516, Leo X made him governor of Modena, and in 1517, of Reggio. It was the beginning of a long and distinguished career in the Papal administration, first under Leo X, and then under the second Medici Pope, Clement VII.

When Guicciardini left for Spain, he had already written two historical works: his family memoirs and an unfinished *History of Florence* from 1378 to his own time. In this history he had voiced his views on the respective merits of the Medicean and the republican regime; and his strictures on these, and particularly on the government of Piero Soderini, who became head of the republic in 1502, doubtless reflected the attitude of many aristocrats. During his stay at the Spanish court, he composed a discourse on the reforms by which, in his view, the republican regime could be improved and saved: "I had nearly finished writing it," he notes in his manuscript, "when I heard the news that the Medici had entered Florence." [2] The same manuscript also contains his report on Spain, as well as a collection of twenty-nine maxims, preceded by the note: "In the year 1512, while I was ambassador in Spain." [3] This is the second of the two earliest collections of his *Ricordi*; the first, which consisted of thirteen maxims, was also written in Spain. Both collections are introduced by an entry which provides a kind of title—the present one was probably adopted only after Guicciardini's death—as well as an explanation of the origin of the reflections contained in them: "Although leisure alone does not give birth to whims, it is indeed true that there can be no whims without leisure." Composed in the relative leisure of his Spanish embassy, about half of these earliest *ricordi* deal with the political conditions of a city-republic, and several of them with questions discussed in the *Discourse of Logrogno,* and in that on Medicean reforms written shortly afterwards; they almost read like by-products of his thinking on the contemporary problems of his native city, for which there was no place in his treatises. After his return from Spain, Guicciardini wrote many new *ricordi,* and in 1528, "during the great leisure I then had," he made another collection of them, containing 181 reflections; this had probably been preceded by an earlier one, which is no longer extant. In May 1530, when his enforced leisure was drawing to an end, he began to compile his final collection of 221 *ricordi.*

In rearranging—usually with greater or lesser changes of their wording—earlier *ricordi*, in combining or omitting others, and in adding new ones, Guicciardini clearly applied to his various collections some principles of order. Yet basically the *Ricordi* remain what they had been from the beginning, namely, reflections on a large number of questions based on Guicciardini's personal experience rather than on any theoretical plan. Thus the successive collections reflect Guicciardini's attitudes to

[2] Francesco Guicciardini, *Dialogo e discorsi del reggimento di Firenze,* ed. R. Palmarocchi (Bari, 1932), p. 218, n. 1 (the discourse on pp. 218–59). Shortly afterwards, he wrote a second discourse (ibid., pp. 260–66), this time on the reforms to be adopted by the Medici.

[3] Raffaele Spongano, *Ricordi, edizione critica* (Firenze, 1951), p. xvi, n. 1.

changing situations. The earliest are full of references to the
political problems of the republican regime in Florence, which
foundered in 1512. But then the horizon widens: the stage is
now set in the Papal State and in Italy at large, at a time of
crisis, when the entry of European powers into Italian politics
had profoundly upset long-established patterns of political behavior; and the writer is no longer the unexperienced ambassador of the Florentine republic, but the successful Papal
governor, used to positions of high responsibility and great
danger. Finally, the scene shifts back to Florence; having been
appointed in 1526 Papal lieutenant-general with the army of
the League of Cognac against Charles V, Guicciardini helped
protect his city from the army of German mercenaries which
threatened it in 1527; and he returned to Florence, where, after
the sack of Rome by that army, the Medici had once more been
expelled and the republican regime restored. Suspect owing to
his close association with them, he fled in September 1529 to
the Papal court. From there he followed the city's staunch resistance against the besieging imperialist army, which ended in
August 1530 with Florence's capitulation, and with the fall of
its last republican regime. It was in May of the same year that
Guicciardini had begun the final collection of his *ricordi*—at
a time, as he writes in the first of them, when the Florentines
had "fought off these armies from their walls for seven months,
though no one would have believed they could do it for seven
days." (C 1).

Like the first collections of *ricordi*, those of 1528 and 1530
belong to periods when the circumstances of Guicciardini's life
provided him with the leisure in which to dedicate himself to
study and writing. In 1528, he began his second, equally unfinished *History of Florence* (the so-called *Cose fiorentine*); probably in 1530, he wrote his *Observations on Machiavelli's Discourses*. Like many other statesmen before and after him,
Guicciardini used such periods of enforced leisure to meditate
on past and present events, to analyse or justify his part in
them, and to search for theoretical solutions of contemporary
problems. They also gave him an opportunity to sift and collect
observations jotted down at random during periods of intense

activity: all but ten of the 181 *ricordi* of the collection of 1528
had been composed before 1525. Indeed, while sustained literary
efforts demanded prolonged periods of freedom from public
activities, the literary form of the brief observation or maxim
lent itself particularly well to a life dominated by political
business.

One may ask why Guicciardini undertook to compile the
successive selections of these maxims—a work that involved a
great deal of rewriting and rearranging. Like his diaries and
family memoirs, they were hardly intended for publication;
even the last of these collections, that of 1530, contains references to his family which were clearly meant for its members.[4]
The keeping of diaries and commonplace books was a Florentine tradition of long standing, and Guicciardini himself dedi-
cated his family memoirs of 1508 to his descendants. Such writings often included advice of a moral or economic character,
along the lines of the treatises on practical wisdom and on
household government which were so popular in fourteenth-
and fifteenth-century Florence. On a vastly superior intellectual
level and with a much wider perspective, Guicciardini's *Ricordi*
could serve a similar purpose. Nor is this only a matter of the
use to which the *ricordi* could be put. Several of them contain
views that were common property of Florentine Renaissance
society and that could also be found expressed, in a simpler
and homelier form, in such handbooks of practical advice as
Paolo da Certaldo's *Libro di buoni costuni*,[5] or in Giovanni
Rucellai's *Zibaldone*.[6] But times had changed: the guidance
which Rucellai gave his sons around the middle of the fifteenth
century presupposed a vigorous civic society whose structure
was still basically intact. Guicciardini, on the other hand, writes
in a time of crisis and disillusionment, when ancient traditions
and institutions had been uprooted or swept away, and when
individual self-reliance and self-preservation, by means fair or
foul, were at a premium. His *Ricordi* show his reactions to the

---

[4] See C 39: *"nostro padre"* instead of *"mio padre"* in the corresponding
ricordo B 66.

[5] Ed. A. Schiaffini (Florence, 1945).

[6] Ed. A. Perosa (London, 1960).

changing contemporary world, as well as to his personal vicissitudes and problems. In this close relationship with his life of
action and his everyday experience, they also reflect an outstanding characteristic of his political thinking.

For Guicciardini's political ideas did not originate primarily
from theoretical study, but from his reactions to the political
situations that confronted him; and if he owed a debt to earlier
political thought, it was to that which was embodied in Florentine political tradition rather than to that expounded in classi-
cal or medieval philosophy. Although acquainted with Plato's
and Aristotle's political theories, as anyone who had received
a humanist education in Florence at the end of the fifteenth
century was bound to be, he disclaimed any scholarly ambitions
—"According to my father's wishes," he says in his diary, "I
pursued, in my early youth, literary studies, and apart from
Latin, I acquired a little Greek, which, however, because of
different occupations, I forgot after a few years."[7] He often
inveighs against abstract theorizing and the mechanical appli-
cation of the political doctrines of antiquity to modern situations. This close connection between political fact and theory
is already shown in his first *History of Florence*, of c. 1509,
where the examination of political conditions and developments,
first under the Medici and then under the new republican
regime established in 1494, led him to formulate general judge-
ments on political questions. Conversely, when in 1512 he tried
to give to his views on the political problems of the republican
regime a systematic form, he was concerned with questions that
had direct relevance to the political situation of contemporary
Florence. While criticisms of republican politics in general, and
of the Gonfalonier of Justice Piero Soderini in particular, which
we already find in the *History of Florence*, are repeated and
elaborated, they are now accompanied by constructive proposals,
such as the limitation of the Gonfalonier's powers and the creation of an aristocratic senate on the Venetian model. Although
as a practical program of reform, the *Discourse of Logrogno*
was obsolete by the time Guicciardini had finished writing it,
it retained its importance as the first comprehensive and sys-

[7] *Scritti autobiografici*, pp. 53–54.

tematic formulation of his views on what constituted good republican government for Florence. The basic assumptions underlying these views are, firstly, that in Florence no good government can exist unless the aristocrats are given a prominent, though not an exclusive, share in it, thus at the same time satisfying their rightful claims and giving power to those who are, by upbringing and status, qualified to wield it; and, secondly, that such government could be established and safeguarded by a judicious combination of constitutional elements. While the former view reflects traditional attitudes of the Florentine patriciate, the latter testifies to the deep-rooted Florentine belief in the effectiveness of institutional policies and reforms. That this belief might occasionally be backed by references to Aristotle's teachings only shows that the *Politics* could once again be read as a practical manual of city-state politics. But Guicciardini's conclusion that the best constitution for Florence was a mixture of monarchical, oligarchical, and democratic elements, while influenced by Aristotle's doctrine of the mixed constitution, is arrived at through an examination of the political conditions of contemporary Florence; if anything, it was this objective and empirical examination of the historical development and present structure of Florentine politics which incidentally confirm for him the validity of Aristotle's theory.

After the Medici restoration, Guicciardini turned his attention to the question of how best to secure the new regime, first in a brief discourse composed while he was still in Spain, and subsequently, in 1516, in a longer one. To accuse him of opportunism would be easy enough; indeed, like so many of his compatriots, including the republican Machiavelli, Guicciardini was, from the beginning, eager to serve the new masters. Yet irrespective of personal interests and commitments, these two discourses reveal a striking continuity of approach to the problem of good government. In the first, Guicciardini shows himself opposed to a regime exclusively founded on the support of partisans, and in favour of giving the people, "which had tasted, during eighteen years, the sweetness of the republican way of life," [8] as large a share in government and administration

8 *Dialogo e discorsi*, p. 265.

as possible; in the second, he criticizes the Medici for having disappointed their followers and estranged the masses, and urges them to rely on the help and advice of a group of loyal citizens, "whom they ought to encourage to speak freely the truth." [9] While accepting Medici supremacy, Guicciardini thus remains loyal to his aristocratic ideals, and to his belief in a balanced form of government which he had expressed in the *Discourse of Logrogno*. Moderation is, in fact, the keynote of all three of these discourses, a moderation that finds its most emphatic expression in his unqualified condemnation of those men who were advising the Medici to assume absolute power: "they could not take a more pernicious decision." [10]

Nor did Guicciardini's long and distinguished service under two Medici popes lead him to modify substantially his views on what constituted good government for Florence. Some time before the death of Leo X in December 1521, he began yet another treatise on this subject, which he completed under the next Medici Pope, Clement VII, in 1525 or 1526. The *Dialogue on Florentine government* is a far more ambitious work than the preceding ones; in it Guicciardini is no longer concerned with immediate reforms but with a systematic enquiry into the problem of the ideal government for Florence, based on an evaluation of the two constitutions the city had experienced in his own time. His critical comparison between the Medicean regime before 1494 and the republican regime that followed it is, on balance, favourable to the former; and yet the picture of an ideal Florentine constitution, which he draws in the second book of the *Dialogue*, resembles the pattern he had outlined before the fall of the republic in 1512. Guicciardini is clearly at pains to justify so remarkable, and in view of his career surprising, a loyalty to his republican sympathies, as is shown by the three different versions of his preface. The work, he points out, is only meant as an intellectual exercise; it expresses the opinions of the interlocutors of the dialogue, not his own; it is not intended for publication (although in the earliest version of the preface, he still visualizes that this might be possible

9 Ibid., p. 271.
10 Ibid., p. 281.

"before I reach old age"). Did he begin composing the *Dialogue* at a time when, under the rule of Cardinal Giulio de' Medici after 1519, Florentines with republican leanings, among them Machiavelli, were hoping against hope that the Medici might soon be prepared to liberalize their rule? The discovery, in 1522, of a conspiracy against the Medici regime dashed these hopes, and in the following year Cardinal Giulio became Pope Clement VII and imposed his will on Florence with greater determination than ever. *Qui s'excuse, s'accuse*: in the end, Guicciardini had to admit, in no uncertain terms, to the possibility of a clash between his loyalties to the Medici and to his native city. But in this event, he insists, his choice would be clear: his first duty would lie with his city.[11]

Whatever the problem of personal loyalties, there certainly is no ambivalence in the constitutional theory he expounds in the *Dialogue*. Despite the advantages which the Medici regime had brought Florence, Guicciardini emphatically does not consider it the ideal form of government, not even in its relatively mild form under Lorenzo the Magnificent. This he is now more certain than ever to have found in a mixed constitution incorporating a variety of checks and balances; a constitution which, while democratic by virtue of a great council similar to the one established in 1494, and monarchical in respect of the head of the state, appointed, like the Gonfalonier of Justice Piero Soderini in 1502, for life, has as its central element an aristocratic senate. Elected for life, the senate was to hold "the balance between despotism and popular license," and was at the same time designed "to keep satisfied the most capable and best-qualified citizens." [12] At the beginning of the *Dialogue*, Guicciardini insists that he is not concerned with theory but with facts, not with whether a constitution is good in itself, but with what its effects would be in a given historical situation; consequently, the doctrines of political philosophers are irrelevant to his inquiry into the best regime for contemporary Florence.[13] It might be argued, with some justification, that

11 Ibid., 3–6, 295–301.
12 Ibid., p. 118.
13 Ibid., pp. 13 ff.

Guicciardini, while pragmatically rejecting past theory, ends up by formulating one himself, and that his own theory contains a claim to absolute validity that is not so different from the claims of political philosophers such as Plato.[14] However, it should be remembered that Guicciardini's approach to politics had from the beginning been empirical and pragmatic rather than theoretical; that his search after an ideal constitution was exclusively concerned with Florence; that his conclusions, however close they sometimes came to Aristotelian concepts, were based on the historical development of that city; and, finally, that he himself made no claim to their universal applicability.

When, in May 1527, the Medici having been once more expelled from Florence, the republican regime was restored for the last time, it was so in a form that was even further removed from Guicciardini's ideals than the one it had possessed until 1512. His personal misfortunes undoubtedly deepened his disappointment over the new regime; having lost, after the sack of Rome and Clement VII's imprisonment in Castel Sant' Angelo, his post as the Pope's lieutenant-general in the army of the League, he was, after his return to Florence, burdened with heavy taxes, and, despite his vast political and diplomatic experience, bypassed in the appointments to civic offices. The problem of divided loyalties, of which he had been so keenly aware in his *Dialogue on Florentine Government*, now proved to have more drastic effects on his life than he could have foreseen when he wrote that work. While he had then put the loyalty to his city above that to his Papal employer, he now forcibly appeared to the republican radicals of 1527 as the faithful servant of two Medici Popes, to the extent of being accused of having, as early as 1512, plotted the Medicean restoration. He found some comfort in the reflection that "the suspicion with which the people regards you, because it considers you a supporter of the Medici, will pass away, and the time will come, and perhaps sooner than you imagine, when you will be held in high esteem"; and that it will then be easier to convince the people "that you are not opposed to a free government." [15]

---

[14] See V. de Caprariis, *Francesco Guicciardini. Dalla politica alla storia* (Bari, 1950), pp. 80 ff.

[15] "Consolatoria" (Sept. 1527), in *Scritti autobiografici*, pp. 179, 180.

But despite his friendship with the head of the state, the Gonfalonier of Justice Niccolò Capponi, these hopes proved vain. Capponi's fall from office in April 1529, when it was discovered that he had been secretly negotiating with the Pope, compromised Guicciardini's position further; and when the Papal and imperial army was advancing on Florence, he fled, in September 1529, to the Papal court. Here may have been a plan to arrest him, together with other friends of the Medici, as he asserted after his flight; in fact, he was condemned in his absence as a rebel. He returned to Florence after the city's capitulation and the restoration of the Medici in August 1530, as Papal representative, and in this capacity, he took a leading share in the persecution of Clement's republican enemies. It was not surprising that he should now support the Medicean regime more wholeheartedly than he had done after 1512. True, despite the ruthless advice he gave the new rulers, in his memoranda of 1530–32, on how to establish their power permanently, he still warned, as he had done in 1516, against the creation of a principality.[16] Yet he materially helped Duke Alessandro de' Medici to consolidate, in 1532, his new princely authority, and later enjoyed great influence under him. After Alessandro's assassination in 1537, when there was a good chance of restoring the republic, Guicciardini was instrumental in securing Cosimo I's succession to the ducal throne. But even now, his vain attempt to impose limitations on Cosimo's authority showed both his belief in constitutional safeguards and his dislike of extreme forms of government. If he had hoped to guide the young ruler, he was soon disillusioned, and virtually retired from public affairs, devoting the last years of his life— he died on 22 May 1540—to his greatest work, the *History of Italy*.

Just as his first *History of Florence* grew out of his researches into the history of his family, also his last work has autobiographical overtones, its original nucleus being an account of his lieutenantship with the army of the League of Cognac. From his family memoirs, Guicciardini had turned to the history of

[16] *Opere inedite*, ed. G. Canestrini (Florence, 1857–67), II, 373. Cf. F. Gilbert, "Alcuni discorsi di uomini politici fiorentini . . . ," in *Archivio Storico Italiano*, XCIII, 2 (1935), 3–24.

his city; from that of the war against Emperor Charles V after 1525, he turned to the history of his country, beginning with the origins of the foreign invasions which had changed its destiny. Nor does his narrative stop at the frontiers of Italy: that country having become the chief stage for the conflicts between France and the Habsburgs, Guicciardini's *History of Italy* time and again assumes the character of a history of Europe.

This extension of Guicciardini's subject reflects, in its turn, the broadening of his personal experience of contemporary affairs. While his juvenile *History of Florence* shows his knowledge of and concern with the politics of his city, the *History of Italy*, written about thirty years later, reveals the vast and manifold experience of an Italian statesman and diplomatist who for many years had been in close touch with the inner counsels of Italian politics, and who more than once had taken a leading part in shaping them. But while the years spent in high office and in the midst of far-reaching political and military events had immeasurably widened and deepened Guicciardini's experience of public affairs, they had also brought him many disappointments; and the pessimistic overtones of his *History of Italy* bear witness to the impact of Italy's misfortunes on the intellectual development of an Italian historian and patriot in an age of crisis.

The development of Guicciardini's views on Italy coincides largely with the time of his friendship with Machiavelli. The two men shared the same views on a number of subjects; yet this went hand in hand with fundamental disagreements. Their intellectual relationship was of the nature of a long debate between equals, rather than of one-sided or mutual influence; while Guicciardini accepted some of the ideas which Machiavelli had put forward in his political works, *The Prince* and the *Discourses*, he strongly rejected others. Dating back to Machiavelli's brief visit, in 1521, to Modena, where Guicciardini was Papal governor, the friendship between the two men became closest in the last years of Machiavelli's life. During the disastrous development of the war of the League of Cognac, Machiavelli was in charge of Florentine fortifications, and went on frequent missions to the Papal lieutenant-general in the dra-

matic months when the army of German *Landsknechte* was
advancing south; and their Florentine and Italian patriotism,
their strenuous efforts to help defend both their city and their
country from the foreign invaders, brought them nearer to one
another than ever. "Io amo messer Francesco Guicciardini, amo
la patria mia più dell' anima," writes Machiavelli a few
weeks before his death in 1527: [17] "I love Francesco Guicciardini and I love my fatherland more than my own soul."

Foremost among the attitudes the two men shared, besides
their patriotism, was an objective and non-ethical approach
to politics, which has earned Guicciardini the epithet of "the
first of the Machiavellians." [18] Where their views differed, as in
the question of the applicability of precedents from Roman
antiquity to modern times, or in that of the intrinsic goodness
or evil of human nature, Guicciardini's objections were largely
bound up with his distrust of Machiavelli's tendency to theorize
and to draw what he would consider to be sweeping conclusions
from inadequate evidence. These objections to some of Machiavelli's basic theories appear already, together with a good deal
of similarity in judgment, in the *Dialogue on Florentine Government*. A few years later, he formulated them systematically
in his unfinished *Observations on the "Discourses" of Machiavelli*, written probably in 1530, when that work was being
prepared for printing. That Guicciardini should have felt the
urge to clarify his views on Machiavelli's political philosophy
is significant in that it shows how deeply Machiavelli's ideas
affected him. For us, the *Observations* have the additional sig-
nificance that Guicciardini was writing them about the time
when he was engaged in compiling the final selection of his
Ricordi.

II

While the *Observations* provide Guicciardini with an opportunity to state his own views in critical examination of those

[17] Letter of April 16, 1527, to Francesco Vettori, in Machiavelli, *Lettere*,
ed. F. Gaeta (Milan, 1961), p. 505.
[18] R. Ridolfi, *Vita di Francesco Guicciardini* (Rome, 1960), p. 214.

of Machiavelli, the *Ricordi* are free from any limitation to a
specific subject. The harvest of an active life by a profound
and subtle mind, they reflect the vicissitudes of that life as well
as the development of his thought. Written over a period of
about eighteen years, stretching from his first high office to his
involuntary retirement from a great public career, they reveal,
both in the addition of new maxims and in the alteration of
earlier ones, the development of his views and the effect on
them of changing external circumstances. That some of these
views should also be expressed in the political treatises written
during that period is not surprising.[19] In fact, many *ricordi*
could have formed the subject of systematic discussions; however, Guicciardini chose to leave them in the lapidary form of
reflections. Adverse to abstract theory which was not based
upon experience, he considered himself, when writing down his
meditations on a wide variety of subjects, primarily a man of
action; and when he finally withdrew from public life, he chose
history and not philosophy as his principal field of activity.

While it would thus be futile to expect to find systematic
order in the *Ricordi*, it would be equally mistaken to deny them
any form of organization. A comparison between the different
collections he made of them, and particularly between the two
last ones of 1528 and 1530, shows Guicciardini attempting, however loosely, to arrange his reflections in groups, with one
ricordo often leading up to another. Taken together, these
groups of *ricordi* cover a number of fairly well-definable topics,
while a few themes, such as that of the function of reason in
human action, run through the entire work. Guicciardini's
basic assumption, that experience was a more reliable source
of knowledge than deductive theory, affected in its turn both

19 To give three examples, which could be easily multiplied: C 134, on
the basic goodness of man, which goes back to the earliest collection of
1512, appears also in the *Discourse of Logrogno* of that year and again in
the *Dialogue on Florentine Government (Dialogo e discorsi*, pp. 225, 55);
C 97 ("che e pochi e non e molti danno communemente el moto alle cose"),
which is also contained in B 30, corresponds to a view stated twice in that
Discourse (pp. 238, 242); the statement, in C 48, that "tutti [gli stati] . . .
sono violenti" by origin, already in B 95, can also be found in the same
Discourse and in the *Dialogue* (pp. 222, 163).

the subject matter of single *ricordi* and the modifications and additions made in the successive collections. Many of the *ricordi* have a direct bearing on the political situation of the day and on Guicciardini's attitude to it; others reflect his experience in peace and war as a high-ranking administrator. Thus, most of the earliest reflections refer, as we have seen, to the Florentine republican regime which fell in 1512. These are included in the collection of 1528, which Guicciardini compiled in the year after the republican restoration, but are nearly all omitted from the last collection of 1530 (C), which Guicciardini began at a time when he was an exile from the Florentine republic. The collection of 1528 (B) is headed by the following remark: "Written before 1525 in other notebooks, but copied in this one at the beginning of the year 1528, during the great leisure I then had, together with most of those [*ricordi*] that follow in this notebook." There has been some scholarly discussion about the meaning of the first words in this sentence; and it may well be that they partly refer to an intermediate collection, made between 1512 and 1525, of which the manuscript is lost.[20] At the same time, there can be no doubt that two of the notebooks mentioned by Guicciardini are identical with the two earliest extant collections of *ricordi* of 1512 (Q^1 and Q^2): of the first twenty-three *ricordi* of B, all but one are, with greater or lesser modifications, taken over from the earliest collections, which contained thirteen and twenty-nine *ricordi* respectively. This combination of an earlier and a later stratum in the 1528 collection is reflected in a change of subject matter which takes place after the first twenty-three *ricordi*: there is a marked shift from civic problems related to the Florentine republic, to questions concerning diplomacy (B 24), the conduct of war (B 28), and the administration of the Papal State (B 29)— in other words, to questions that would have a direct bearing on Guicciardini's experience, first as ambassador in Spain, and then as Papal administrator. Similarly, the final collection, which Guicciardini began to compile in May 1530, opens with

[20] This is the thesis of the editor of the *Ricordi*, R. Spongano; see his preface, pp. xvi ff. The biographer of Guicciardini, Roberto Ridolfi, did not consider it to be definitively proven; see his *Vita*, pp. 485–6.

a long new *ricordo* on the siege of Florence by the Imperialists,
which at that time had lasted seven months (C 1). In this
reflection, Guicciardini considers the impact of faith on the resistance put up by the Florentines, which had prolonged the
struggles beyond all rational expectation; and several of the
newly added *ricordi* in that collection deal with the interven-
tion of imponderable factors in the course of events, which
often renders rational prediction futile,[21] or specifically discuss
the effectiveness of religious belief in political and military
affairs.[22] Although meditations along similar lines can also occasionally be found earlier,[23] the dramatic events which Guicciardini was witnessing during the months of Florence's heroic
resistance provided him with fresh evidence for the fallibility
of reason in foretelling the vagaries of individual and collective
action.

But if new experiences could confirm as well as refute pre-
viously held opinions, they could also modify them in details
or bring about qualifications or changes in emphasis. Such
changes could affect the form as well as the content of single
ricordi; and changes in form were for Guicciardini a matter
of intellectual clarity and penetration rather than of stylistic
elegance. A comparison of the different versions of single *ricordi*
shows his efforts to achieve conciseness and lucidity of expression. In the process some *ricordi* might be ruthlessly omitted,
new ones added, or several *ricordi* fused into one. It is not
always easy to determine whether, in a given case, changes are
caused by this striving after concise and lucid formulation or
by Guicciardini's having modified his views on the subject.
Thus C 41 combines into one, four or five earlier *ricordi* on
the necessity of harsh and cruel measures, *severità*, in government. Was this because his view on this question had mellowed,
as the editor of the *Ricordi* suggests,[24] or simply because
Guicciardini wished to avoid repetition? At the same time,

21 See C 81, 116, 117, 136, 166, 180.
22 See C 124.
23 See B 28, 127.
24 P. x. I am not certain that he is right in believing that B 12 had been
used for this *ricordo*.

clarity and brevity of statement did not necessarily imply for him finality of judgment. The tentative, almost groping character of many of the *ricordi* seems to reveal a search after truths that might elude precise and rigid formulations. The same reluctance to commit himself definitively may also help to explain apparent inconsistencies, such as his wavering between an optimistic belief in the fundamental goodness of human nature, and a pessimistic conviction that, in reality, most men are wicked (C 134, 201). The *ricordo* stating that "there are more bad men than good" (C 201) is added to the collection of 1530, doubtless under the influence of Guicciardini's recent personal experiences; yet while this may reveal a significant shift in his view on this matter, equally significant is his retention of the optimistic belief in human goodness (C 134), a belief that already appears in the first collection of 1512 (Q^{1-2} 4) and, in almost identical terms, in the *Discourse of Logrogno*,[25] that is voiced again in the *Dialogue on Florentine Government*,[26] and is included in the collection of 1528 (B 3), where it is further stressed by the addition of a new *ricordo,* equally taken over in 1530, to the effect that of a man who prefers evil to goodness "you may surely say that he is a beast, not a man" (B 4, C 135).

There is perhaps no better example of Guicciardini's reluctance to commit himself than his discussion of the question of the validity of general rules of conduct—and hence, ultimately, of the *ricordi* themselves. "Read these *ricordi* often, and ponder them well," warns the ninth *ricordo* of the final collection. "For it is easier to know and understand them than to put them into practice." Guicciardini adds to the corresponding reflection of the collection of 1528 the explanation that this difficulty in carrying out rules of conduct is due to man's failure to let knowledge guide his actions—"for very often, men will not act on their knowledge" (B 100). From the beginning, Guicciardini had voiced his doubts about the existence of generally valid rules of action. Already in the second collection of 1512 he had said of rules (*regole*) that "they are written

25 Op. cit., p. 225.
26 Op. cit., p. 55.

in books"; but "exceptional cases are written in your discretion" (Q^2 12). This *ricordo* is included in an expanded form in the collection of 1528, together with a new one to the same effect (B 35, 121), which is then omitted in that of 1530. In the final version, Guicciardini insists even more strongly that discretion (*discrezione*), the pragmatic judgment of each case on its own merits, may, in the end, matter far more than theoretical rules; for "in nearly all [things], one must make distinctions and exceptions, because of the differences in their circumstances" (C 6). Similarly, he adds in 1530 to a *ricordo* of 1528 the observation that "you cannot always abide by a fixed rule of conduct" (C 186), and emphasizes even more strongly the superiority of discretion over theory: "In this, as in all other matters, you must be able to distinguish the character of the person, of the case, of the occasion; and for that, discretion is necessary. If discretion is not given by nature, it can rarely be learned from experience. It can never be learned from books." Rules, experience, discretion—these are, for Guicciardini, three possible guides of action; and while experience proves time and again superior to theory, often natural "tact" only will suffice. Guicciardini evidently does not see any inherent contradiction between such casuistic pragmatism and the claim that his maxims contained useful guidance. The limited applicability of general rules, owing to the innumerable exceptions to which in practice they are subject, does not deprive them altogether of their validity, just as the power of fortune does not entirely prevent reason and free will from influencing man's destinies.

Accordingly, Guicciardini sees the question of the usefulness of general rules of conduct as part of the wider problem of the place of reason in the sphere of human action. One of the principal themes of the *Ricordi*, this wider question plays a key role in Guicciardini's, as in Machiavelli's, thought. In spite of Guicciardini's deepening scepticism on this subject, he again appears reluctant to commit himself definitively. Thus in C 137 —a new *ricordo* added in 1530—he voices much the same confidence in the superiority, in politics, of reason over ignorance, which had been an underlying theme of his *Dialogue on Florentine Government*. Yet in the preceding *ricordo*, equally added in 1530 and referring to the siege of Florence in that year, he points out that "it sometimes happens that fools do greater things than wise men" (C 136). This, he says, is due to the fact that the wise men take little account of fortune, whose effects can sometimes be "incredible"; and he inserts, after these two new *ricordi*, an earlier one from the collection of 1528 that adds a determinist note: "Neither fools nor wise men can ultimately resist what must be" (C 138, B 80). Fundamentally a rationalist, Guicciardini is increasingly convinced of the limitations of reason in the conduct of human affairs, without, however, abandoning his aristocratic belief in the superiority of knowledge over ignorance. Indeed, his very scepticism regarding the effectiveness of reason is largely based on a rational analysis of past and present events. In the great debate on the respective role of *fortuna* and *virtù*, of fortune and individual initiative, which so strikingly reflects the intellectual and political crisis of early sixteenth-century Italy, Guicciardini consequently adopts a less optmistic approach than his friend Machiavelli, although it must be added that also Machiavelli's attitude to this problem was, in the long run, more tentative and liable to change than might appear from the reading of *The Prince*. But for Guicciardini, who sometimes tends to oversimplify Machiavelli's views in order to make his own position clearer, Machiavelli stands for the belief in the effectiveness of reason and hence in the possibility of an exact political science; and he comments scathingly that "in affairs of state, you should guide yourself not so much by what reason demonstrates a prince ought to do, as by what he will most likely do, according to his nature or habits. Princes will often do what they please or what they know, and not what they should" (C 128). This observation, if accepted, would demolish the very foundations of *The Prince* as a guide to political action; just as, on a different plane, Guicciardini's scepticism about the relevance for contemporary politics of examples from Roman antiquity strikes at another basic assumption of Machiavelli's political theory.[27]

27 See C 110. Cf. also the *Dialogue on the Government of Florence*, op. cit., p. 68, and the *Considerazioni intorno ai Discorsi di Machiavelli sopra la prima Deca di Tito Livio*, in *Scritti politici e Ricordi*, ed. R. Palmarocchi (Bari, 1933), p. 11.

For Guicciardini, as for Machiavelli, the problem of *fortuna* and *virtù* applied both to the interpretation of historical events and to the conduct of personal affairs. If in his historical writings Guicciardini might observe the working of fortune in history, in the *Ricordi* he concentrates on its place in human affairs in general. In so far as fortune's power limited the predictability of events, it severely handicapped any attempt to lay down valid rules of conduct. "If you consider the matter carefully, you cannot deny that Fortune has great power over human affairs. We see these affairs constantly being affected by fortuitous circumstances that men could neither foresee nor avoid," he says in *ricordo* 30. Guicciardini's scathing criticism of astrological claims to predict events contrasts with the deep-rooted Renaissance belief in that "science" (C 57, 207): "How wisely the philosopher spoke," he observes in *ricordo* 58, "when he said: 'Of future contingencies there can be no determined truth' "; and he sums up his view on this matter in *ricordo* 23: "The future is so deceptive and subject to so many accidents that very often even the wisest of men is fooled when he tries to predict it." Accordingly, it is prudent, "although a future event may seem inevitable, never [to] depend upon it completely" (C 81); just as it is futile (*fallacissimo*) to hope to learn—as Machiavelli had been trying to do—from the past for the future: for "every tiny, particular circumstance that changes is apt to alter a conclusion" (C 114). What matters, in the end, is once more discretion (*discrezione*)—the discerning judgment of each event on its own merits.

With such reservations and uncertainties, which in their turn form an essential part of his rational philosophy based on experience, Guicciardini presents in the *Ricordi* the elements of a theory of conduct. The central topic of this work is the preservation and aggrandizement of the individual and his family in a society dominated by conflicting bids for power and wealth. Guicciardini's exclusive concern is with man as a political animal who would renounce power only if forced to do so (C 17), but the scope of whose actions is constantly determined by his relations with his fellow men. Hence the importance of a proper understanding of the political and social conditions in which man has to act; and accordingly, Guicciardini's comments on contemporary society and politics have time and again direct relevance for the problems of individual behavior. For Guicciardini, the social and political background was that of early sixteenth-century Italy, in which the survival of much of the varied pattern of earlier Renaissance politics went hand in hand with the decline of long-established institutions and with sudden military and political changes. There can have been few Italians of his generation who possessed so wide a knowledge of that society as Giucciardini, who was equally at home at princely courts and republics, and who was intimately familiar with the intricacies of contemporary diplomacy, with the ups and downs of politics and wars, and with the rise and fall of governments. His reflections reveal him as an unbiased and detached observer—a quality that is particularly striking in his *ricordi* on the Church and the Papacy. This high-ranking Papal administrator could still include, in his collection of 1528, a *ricordo* dating back to 1512 in which he expressed his hope that he might see, before he died, "the world delivered from the tyranny of these wicked priests" (B 14, Q^2 17); and although he omits it from his final collection of 1530, he expands it in branding "the avarice and the sensuality of the clergy" in another *ricordo* of 1528 (C 28, B 124).

His condemnation of the Church remains unaffected by his refusal to draw personal consequences from it: "the positions I have held under several popes have forced me, for my own good, to further their interests. Were it not for that, I should have loved Martin Luther more than myself" (C 28). For if Guicciardini considers knowledge of the contemporary world necessary for rational individual behavior, he also considers it a postulate of enlightened self-interest which demands the acceptance of that world as it is. Guicciardini's attitude on this matter comes close to that of Machiavelli, to the extent of sometimes adopting the conditional device with which Machiavelli introduces some of the chapters of *The Prince*: if men were good, this counsel would be wrong; but since most of them are wicked, you have to act toward them as they would act towards you.[28] But not only is Guicciardini far more moderate in the conclusions he draws from such premises, as when he admits the necessity of harsh measures because most men are "either not very good or not very wise," while at the same time expressing his preference for a middle path between *severità* and *dolcezza* (C 41). He is also concerned with giving advice to the subject or citizen rather than to the despotic ruler—that is to men like himself who, although they might be placed in positions of great responsibility and power, would also have to know how to be subject to the rule of others.

We have seen that, in the collection of 1530, nearly all the early maxims on republican politics are omitted. Their place is taken by reflections on the behavior of subjects and princes and their mutual relations. While this shift reflects the vicissitudes of Guicciardini's career, as well as his final estrangement from the republican cause, it also doubtless reveals his growing conviction that the future belonged, in Florence as in most of Italy, to monarchy; and his attitude towards change, like that toward society, shows a pragmatic acceptance of it, whatever his views on its desirability. He advises resolutely against taking an active part in trying to bring about a change of government, "unless he do it out of necessity, or because he hopes to be head of the new government" (C 51); and he condemns participating in conspiracies, not because they are objectively wrong, but because they endanger the lives of the conspirators (C 19, 20). Yet he can speak with evident distaste of tyranny (a term which Machiavelli studiously avoids in *The Prince*) and with admiration of the valor of republican Florence in resisting her enemies.

The man for whom Guicciardini writes his rules of conduct is no longer, like his Florentine forbears, protected by long-established institutions and traditions, as a member of a tightly-knit community; born into a world of conflict and change, of dissolving traditions and fresh opportunities, he has to meet its challenges with a new sense of self-reliance. In order to defend and assert himself against the selfishness of his fellowmen, Guic-

[28] See, e.g., *The Prince*, ch. 16, 18; cf. C 5, 41, 48, 157.

ciardini wants him to act as if he were surrounded by enemies. Although he might prefer to trust them, he must meet them with suspicion, for "men are so false, so insidious, so deceitful and cunning" (C 157); although he would like to be frank and honest toward them, he must simulate and hide his intentions (C 104); [29] although lying is morally reprehensible, he has to practice it (C 37). He must exaggerate his own power (C 86) and cover up his weaknesses (C 196), and above all he must be secretive (C 49); although it is desirable enough to "discuss things with pleasant, loving familiarity," it is prudent not to speak of one's own affairs, "except when necessary" (C 184). His is a harsh world in which revenge on one's enemies is sweet, and may be necessary (C 72, 74), and in which true security consists in a situation in which your enemies, although they wish to do so, are unable to harm you (C 27).

Guicciardini takes it for granted that political power is desirable (C 16); [30] and while deploring indiscriminate egotism, he makes success in this world depend upon enlightened self-interest (C 218).[31] The trouble is that men do not always appreciate where their true interest lies: "to think it always resides in some pecuniary advantage rather than in honor, in knowing how to keep a reputation, and a good name." Indeed, it is desire for honor and glory that both ennobles and sanctions political ambition: the craving after power for its own sake is "pernicious and detestable" (C 32). Such craving, he adds in the final version of 1530, is common among princes. He thus draws, in the light of long years of experience of princely courts and politics, a distinction between the ordinary man and the ruler that retains some of the civic sentiment of the earliest version of this *ricordo* (Q^{1-2} 2).[32] But also his notion of honor, *onore*, is not devoid of civic Florentine overtones: in Florentine administrative terminology, *onori* were the highest posts in the city's government, which did not carry salary, in

29 See also C 37 and 133.
30 See also C 17.
31 Added in 1530.
32 At the same time, the final version omits the reference to the public good from that of 1512.

contrast to the salaried offices of the territorial administration, the *utile*. Thus Guicciardini's declaration, in a *ricordo* of 1528 and 1530 (C 15) that he had always desired *"onore e utile, like all men,"* retains, despite its universal applicability, some of the subtle Florentine distinction between the different motives for seeking positions in the state: social ambition and public-spiritedness, and desire for economic gain.

Reputation (*reputazione*) is one of the basic concepts of the *Ricordi*; time and again, Guicciardini reverts to the desirability of acquiring and preserving it, and to the difficulties in achieving this. "Do not strive harder to gain favor than to keep your good reputation," he says in a new *ricordo* of 1530; for "when you lose your good reputation, you also lose good will, which is replaced by contempt" (C 42). A good name is more important than great wealth (C 158); like Machiavelli, he considers keeping up appearances essential for preserving one's reputation and furthering one's interests: "one of the greatest pieces of good fortune a man can have," he says in a passage that could have been written by the author of *The Prince,* "is the chance to make something he has done in his own interest appear to have been done for the common good" (C 142). But unlike Machiavelli, Guicciardini is thinking of the ordinary member of the sophisticated and self-seeking Renaissance society rather than of the prince; and unlike him he points out, in a *ricordo* retained in all collections, that in the long run only those good appearances which are based on fact will last (C 44).[33] At the same time, he admits in a late *ricordo* that contrary to what he had thought in his youth, such superficial accomplishments as "knowing how to play, dance, and sing, and such trivialities" may help create a good impression, especially at the courts of princes, "for the world and the princes are no longer made as they should be, but as they are" (C 179). Guicciardini, who disliked frivolity [34] and cherished a patrician sobriety, clearly found the sixteenth-century courtier uncongenial; yet he accepts him as part of a new age.

As so many of his *ricordi,* his reflections on reputation and

[33] Cf. Q1-2 3, B 2.
[34] See also C 167, 200.

honor are intensely personal; in them Guicciardini, having been compelled to withdraw from public affairs after the collapse of his career in Papal service, looks back on the motives and aims of his past life; and the charges of fraud that formed the legal pretext for his trial and condemnation by a Florentine court in March 1530 lend to some of the last *ricordi* an additional sense of apologia which echoes the two discourses he wrote in his self-defense in 1527.[35] In this, as in other respects, the final collection of the *ricordi* appears, in retrospect, almost like a political testament: although Guicciardini doubtless hoped that the period of enforced leisure would be no more than an episode in his public career, it actually proved a turning point in his life. After a term as Papal governor of Bologna between 1531 and 1534, a post he lost on the death of Clement VII, he retired more and more to private life and devoted his last years to his greatest historical work, the *History of Italy*. Written down over a period of eighteen years, the *Ricordi* not only express Guicciardini's views on a large number of questions, but also contain the materials for a self-portrait. Some of his self-analysis reminds one of Montaigne: "I have been of a very easy-going nature" (C 132); "I have always been resolute and firm in my actions" (C 156); "like all men, I have pursued honor and profit" (C 15). He scorns frivolity and vanity (C 200), despises ignorance (C 168), and ridicules self-deception (C 122). Ideally he would wish to be able to "do or carry out things perfectly, that is, to have them free of the slightest defect or disorder" (C 126); but he realizes how difficult it is to achieve this. In spite of his doubts concerning the effectiveness of reason in the conduct of human affairs, he has learnt to control his actions by thought (C 83). While he recognizes, like Machiavelli, the power in political life of religious faith, his attitude towards ecclesiastical ritual borders on agnosticism (C 124); [36] what really matters, he says in a late *ricordo,* are not fasts and prayers but Christian charity, "to harm no one, and to help everyone as much as you can" (C 159). At heart a moderate,

---

[35] "Consolatoria" and "Defensoria," in *Scritti autobiografici,* pp. 165–90, 249–81; C 204 clearly refers to the charges of fraudulent practices.
[36] See also C 92.

he admires courage but despises injudicious bravery (C 70, 95), and would like to temper severity with kindness, vengeance with clemency.[37] In the last *ricordo* of the collection of 1528, which he omitted from that of 1530, he accepts and expands Petrarch's verdict on the Florentines: "They are by nature lively and acute rather than grave and mature" (B 181) —qualities that he may well have claimed as his own and that were in fact shared by the Florentine patriciate to which he belonged by birth. For however much his public career had endowed him with an Italian rather than a Florentine perspective, he remained deeply attached to his native city, as well as to the aristocratic attitudes of his class. Adverse to revolutions and prepared to accept existing regimes whatever their nature, he never quite abandoned his belief in reforms from within; thus he says in a *ricordo* of 1528 and 1530: "Whenever a country falls into the hands of a tyrant, I think it the duty of good citizens to try and cooperate with him, and to use their influence to do good and avoid evil" (C 220). Loyalty, to his city or to his masters, clearly mattered a great deal to him; [38] but so did honor, and few *ricordi* have so immediate a ring of personal commitment as the one in which he speaks of his life-long desire for it: "A man who esteems honor highly will succeed in everything, since he takes no account of toil, danger, or money. I have experienced it myself, and therefore I can say it and write it: the actions of men who do not have this burning stimulus are dead and vain" (C 118).

[37] See above, pp. 141.
[38] See above, pp. 98.

Translator's Preface

If Guicciardini's *Ricordi* has been as well known as Machiavelli's *Prince*, they would surely have competed for the reputation of being the most immoral piece of political prose of the early Cinquecento. The great critic Francesco DeSanctis, whose liberal-nationalism generally predisposed him to see the excellence of neglected or little known Italians, called Guicciardini's book of political maxims "the corruption of Italy, codified and exalted to a rule of life." [1] It is easy enough to understand why these cynical, wordly-wise *ricordi*, with their constant and clear appeal to self-interest, might have given offense. But to take Guicciardini to task for divorcing political action from ethics is to miss the point of his particular contribution to the history of political thought. For it was precisely the virtue of his works, and those of his friend Machiavelli, that they finally and completely removed politics from its moorings in ethics and philosophy.

In Guicciardini's world of thought, political and social action is not to be determined by super-temporal ethical, theological, or religious principles; rather, it should be based on self-interest *(el particulare)*, and on reason. To be sure, both require taking cognizance of the demands of honor; but not any longer the chivalric sort of honor. Guicciardini understands honor in the Florentine sense of a duty performed without pay, for which one receives recognition and homage. Honor, in other words, is not an abstraction against which life is molded and measured, but a pragmatic notion, a force like all others, of great—perhaps even primary—importance, but not qualitatively different from the others. And among these others, Guicciardini exalts experience and native ability as necessary prerequisites of proper

[1] Francesco DeSanctis, *Storia della letteratura italiana* (Napoli, 1873), II, p. 118.

33

political action. When these qualities are found properly com-
bined in an individual, they produce discretion, that wonderful
virtue which enables a man to see the way things are, and to
act accordingly.

Guicciardini speaks so often and so emphatically of the need
for experience, that we might be tempted to see in him the
seeds of empiricism. But a careful reading of these *ricordi* will
show that for him the opposition of reason and experience, of
which later generations made so much, simply did not exist.
When he tells us (C 12) that the similarity of proverbs in all
countries is due to the fact that people everywhere have the
same, or similar, experiences, he is simply establishing the
homogeneity of experience, which makes it possible to deal
with matters consistently, rationally, and universally. For him,
experience and reason are simply the two sides of the same
coin. He says explicitly (C 10) that native intelligence, no
matter how great, can get nowhere without the help of experience. On the other hand, learning imposed on weak minds not
only does not better them but tends to hurt them (C 47). In
ricordo B 160 he tells us it is right to act according to rational
principles even if things turn out wrong, and warns us not to
be proud of success if it came about by chance. And then, in
B 70, he again tells us that experience teaches a great deal,
and more to large minds than to small. In short, not only is
there no polarity—not to speak of hostility—between reason
and experience, but they are in fact inseparable, the indispen-
sable prerequisites for knowledge and discretion.

Guicciardini constantly reminds us that Fortune, that irra-
tional and whimsical character, can never be left out of consideration. We can almost see him sighing as he writes:
"Although cleverness and care may accomplish many things,
they are nevertheless not enough. Man also needs good Fortune." (C 30) The value of all those lessons learned from reason
and experience would seem to be rendered nugatory by the
power of blind Fortune over human affairs. But here, too, the
inconsistency is only apparent. Knowledge and discretion may
not be sufficient to assure success in human affairs, but they are
certainly necessary. Like Machiavelli, though less directly, Guic-

ciardini uses mind to restrict the force and the effectiveness of Fortune's blows. "Remember this," he warns, "whoever lives a life of chance will in the end find himself a victim of chance. The right way is to think, to examine, and to consider every detail carefully, even the most minute. Even if you do, it takes great pains to make things come out right. Imagine how things must go for those who drift." (C 187) Clearly, the lesson that Guicciardini wanted his descendants to learn from his *ricordi* was that the forces governing life, especially political life, are knowable and, to a large degree, controlable; and that such knowledge and control require effort, talent, experience, mind —and Fortune.

* * *

Recent students of Guicciardini's *Ricordi* have been more concerned with the dispute concerning their textual tradition than with their intellectual content. The dispute arose only some thirty years ago, and has already produced a number of very learned, highly detailed studies on both sides. There certainly is no need to go into the minutiae of evidence each side has adduced. But the problem poses an interesting challenge to the scholar-detective, and merits being presented here at least in its general outlines.

Basing himself on the autograph manuscripts, Giuseppe Canestrini first published the *Ricordi* in 1857, under the title *Ricordi civili e politici*.[2] Canestrini presented the two series as one, numbered sequentially and with the second series first. The Guicciardini family archives contain two autograph manuscripts of the *ricordi,* subsequently called B and C, the first containing 181 *ricordi,* the latter 221; and two autograph notebooks (*quaderni*), subsequently called Q 1 and Q 2, containing twelve and twenty-nine *ricordi* respectively. All twelve in Q 1 are repeated in Q 2. There is no doubt that both notebooks were written at the time of Guicciardini's embassy to Spain, in 1512. At the head of the series we call B, in Guicciardini's own

---

[2] Francesco Guicciardini, *Opere inedite,* ed. Giuseppe Canestrini (Firenze, 1857-67, 10 vols.), II, pp. 81-224.

hand, there is a note telling us they were "written before 1525 in other notebooks, but copied in this one at the beginning of the year 1528, during the great leisure I then had, together with most of those that follow in this notebook." In *ricordo* B 138, Guicciardini mentions the date at which he is writing, which is February 3, 1523 (Florentine style, i.e., February 3, 1524, our style). And before *ricordo* B 172, he wrote: "Supplement begun in April, 1528." As for series C, it was definitely written in 1530, during and after the siege of Florence. It contains 221 *ricordi*, using 127 from B (combining some, re-casting them all), five from A (about which series more in a moment), and adding ninety-one new ones.

To recapitulate: Guicciardini wrote and re-wrote his *ricordi* several times, changing them, polishing them, and rejecting some versions altogether. If we consider the notebooks Q 1 and Q 2 together, there are three autograph manuscripts of the *Ricordi*: these notebooks of 1512, containing twenty-nine *ricordi*; the manuscript of 1528 (B), containing 181 *ricordi*, 171 of which were written before 1525, and ten added in April, 1528, presumably at the time when Guicciardini was transcribing the whole series from another manuscript which no longer exists; and a manuscript of 1530 (C) containing 221 *ricordi*, ninety-one of which were new, and the rest re-casts of earlier versions.

The dispute arose when Roberto Palmarocchi published his edition of the *Ricordi*,[3] giving the first and second series (B and C) in their chronological sequence, and numbered separately. At about the same time, Michele Barbi published an article [4] in which he tried to show that aside from Q 1 and Q 2, there were really three versions of the *Ricordi*, which he baptized A, B, and C. A, of course, was that manuscript from which Guicciardini copied B in 1528, but which is nowhere to be found. Barbi arrived at his conclusion by comparing the autograph manuscript B with various printed versions and

---

3 Guicciardini, *Ricordi*, in: *Scritti politici e Ricordi*, ed. Roberto Palmarocchi (Bari, 1933).

4 Michele Barbi, "Per una compiuta edizione dei Ricordi civili e politici del Guicciardini," in: *Studi di filologia italiana*, III, pp. 163–196.

manuscripts of the *Ricordi* dating from the latter half of the sixteenth century, conserved in various libraries throughout Italy. The origin of these copies seems clear. One of the manuscripts *Biblioteca Riccardiana* 3.2967) mentions that "Piero Guicciardini, son of Nicholò, gave a copy of these 'admonishments' (*avvertimenti*) to Don Flavio Orsini . . . much to the dismay of the Guicciardini." [5] That very probably happened in 1561. Fifteen years later, a printed edition of the *Ricordi* appeared in Paris, published by Corbinelli.[6] And in 1582, another appeared in Venice, published by Fra Sisto.[7] Many of the extant manuscripts, on the other hand, are hard to date; but they are of the latter half of the sixteenth century, some of the seventeenth, and one may be as early as 1562, just one year after Piero made a gift of the original. The entire dispute revolves around the question whether Piero's gift was simply a copy of B, or another manuscript from which Guicciardini copied B. Barbi, and Raffaele Spongano after him, fervently affirm the existence of A.[8] They point out that the motto and the first twenty-three *ricordi* of B are, with only one exception, re-writes of the twenty-nine *ricordi* in Q 2. And the *ricordi* from B 24 to B 171 correspond nearly completely to the first 147 of the *ricordi* in A (which contains in all 161). What could be more logical than to suppose that Guicciardini sat down in April, 1528 with Q 2 and A before him, and transcribed both into B making only a few changes, and adding ten new *ricordi*?

To Palmarocchi, the matter did not seem quite so logical at all. If things are as Barbi claims, he asks, why is it that B 172 (the first of the supplement begun after April, 1528) appears as A 155) Furthermore, he says, "if it is true that A 1 corresponds

---

[5] Raffaele Spongano, *Ricordi, edizione critica* (Firenze, 1951), p. XXI, n. 1.

[6] Under the title *Più consigli et avvertimenti di M. Fr. Guicciardini Gentilhuomo fior. in materia di re publica et di privata* (Paris, 1576).

[7] Under the title *Considerazioni civili sopra l'Historie di M. Francesco Guicciardini e d'altri historici. Trattate per modo di discorso da M. Remigio Fiorentino* (Venezia, 1582).

[8] So, too, does the excellent critic Mario Fubini, in "Le quattro redazioni dei *Ricordi* del Guicciardini," in: *Studi sulla letteratura del Rinascimento* (Firenze, 1948), pp. 138–207.

to B 24, it is also true that five [actually, six] of the first twenty-three *ricordi* in B are also to be found in A, though in a different order." [9] He finally points out that of the final eleven *ricordi* in A none except 155 is to be found in B, but that many re-appear in C. If B had been transcribed from Q 2 and A, it hardly seems likely that Guicciardini would have omitted the last eleven *ricordi* of A, only to pick some of them up two years later, when writing C.

In 1951, Raffaele Spongano published his critical edition of the *Ricordi,* which is a masterpiece of erudition. By comparing all the manuscripts, several of which he uncovered, by making the most detailed linguistic and editorial analysis of the various versions, he succeeds in showing that a manuscript A did indeed exist. His presentation, if not iron-clad, is most convincing. But since I proposed only to outline the problem and not to solve it, and since an even modest attempt to present Spongano's case would require going into the minute details I promised to avoid, I feel justified in stating only his conclusion, without the proofs. Suffice it to say, then, that on the basis of present evidence, it would seem that Guicciardini wrote four versions of his *Ricordi.*

Nevertheless, the text of A differs so little from B that it would hardly have been worth reproducing it here. I have translated C, B, and Q 2, and given them in that order, which is the reverse of the chronological. C is the most mature, the most thought-out version. It seemed to me that it should be read first so that the others might be measured against it. To facilitate comparisons, I have included a table of correspondences among the various versions. I have also added a few footnotes in the hope that they will illuminate the text.

I wish to thank my colleagues and friends Carlo Ascheri and Eduardo Saccone for their invaluable help in penetrating to the meaning of some of Guicciardini's hard, terse language. For all errors, I am, of course, solely responsible.

MARIO DOMANDI

Vassar College
June, 1964

[9] Palmarocchi, *Scritti politici e Ricordi,* p. 372.

Series C

1. THE PIOUS say that faith can do great things, and, as the gospel tells us, even move mountains. The reason is that faith breeds obstinacy. To have faith means simply to believe firmly—to deem almost a certainty—things that are not reasonable; or, if they are reasonable, to believe them more firmly than reason warrants. A man of faith is stubborn in his beliefs; he goes his way, undaunted and resolute, disdaining hardship and danger, ready to suffer any extremity.

Now, since the affairs of the world are subject to chance and to a thousand and one different accidents, there are many ways in which the passage of time may bring unexpected help to those who persevere in their obstinacy. And since this obstinacy is the product of faith, it is then said that faith can do great things.

In our own day, the Florentines offer an excellent example of such obstinacy. Contrary to all human reason, they prepared for an attack by the pope and the emperor,[1] even though they had no hope of help from any quarter, were disunited, and burdened with thousands of other difficulties. And they have fought off these armies from their walls for seven months, though no one would have believed they could do it for seven days. Indeed, the Florentines have managed things in such a manner that, were they to win, no one would be surprised;

[1] G. is referring to the siege of Florence conducted by the Imperialist General Philibert, prince of Orange. Charles V had become master of Italy through the Peace of Cambrai (August 5, 1529) and had concluded a "perpetual league" with the Medici pope, Clement VII. The Florentines preferred to resist both the emperor and the pope, rather than allow the Medici to return. Their gallant and nearly successful resistance was broken after eight months. They surrendered on August 12, 1530. The Medici returned, and Alessandro, natural son of Lorenzo, duke of Urbino, became hereditary duke.

whereas earlier, everyone had considered them lost. And this obstinacy is largely due to the faith that they cannot perish, according to the prediction of Brother Jerome of Ferrara.[2]

* * *

2. SOME PRINCES confide to their ambassadors all their secret intentions, and tell them the goals they intend to achieve in their negotiations with the other princes. Others deem it better to tell their ambassador only as much as they want the other prince to believe. For if they wish to deceive, it seems almost necessary to deceive first their own ambassador, the agent and instrument who must deal with and convince the other prince. Each of these opinions has its reason. On the one hand, an ambassador who knows his prince means to deceive will hardly be able to speak and treat as warmly, effectively, and firmly as he would if he believed the negotiations were sincere and not fake. Furthermore, either levity or ill will might cause him to reveal the intentions of his prince—and that an ambassador ignorant of the truth could not do. On the other hand, it often happens that an ambassador who believes his false instructions to be genuine will be more insistent than the matter requires. For if he believes his prince really wishes to achieve a specific end, he will not be as moderate and circumspect in his negotiations as he would have been had he known the truth. It is impossible to give ambassadors instructions so detailed as to cover every circumstance; rather discretion must teach them to accommodate themselves to the end generally being pursued. But if the ambassador does not fully know that end, he cannot pursue it, and therefore he may err in a thousand ways.

In my opinion, a prince who has prudent and honest ambassadors, well-disposed toward him, and well-provided for, so that they have no reason to depend on others, would do better to reveal his intentions. But if he cannot be sure that his ambassadors completely fit this description, it is safer to leave them ignorant and to let the grounds for convincing others be the same grounds that convince the ambassadors themselves.

* * *

2 Brother Jerome is, of course, Savonarola.

3. EXPERIENCE SHOWS that even a great prince finds well-qualified ministers to be very rare. If the prince were not a good judge of men, or if he were too stingy to pay them well, no one would be surprised that such a shortage existed. But if a prince be free of these two defects, one may well wonder why well-qualified ministers should be rare, considering that men of all ranks are anxious to serve him; and that there are so many opportunities for reward from such service.

This state of affairs will not seem strange to anyone who studies it carefully. For the minister of a prince—I speak now of those ministers who serve in important capacities—must needs be a man of extraordinary ability; and such men are rare. Furthermore, he must be a man of great loyalty and integrity; and such men are even rarer. And if it is hard to find men who fulfill one of these two prerequisites, how much harder to find those who fulfill both! A prudent prince, one who does not want to face tasks as they arise daily, will foresee these difficulties and provide for them by choosing as ministers men as yet untrained. By testing them in various matters, and by rewarding them, he will make them expert and faithful. For though it is difficult to find men who already possess these qualities, one can certainly hope to produce them with time.

It is easy to see why secular princes who apply themselves diligently should be better furnished with ministers than the popes are. Since the secular prince generally lives longer than the pope, and since he is succeeded by someone very much like himself, men respect him more and have better hopes of lasting in his service—especially since the successor to a secular prince can easily trust those who have been used, or were beginning to be used, by his predecessor. Furthermore, the ministers of a secular prince are either his subjects or they have been rewarded with properties that are in his domain; and thus they must necessarily respect or fear him and his successors.

But these rules do not apply to the popes, since they generally do not live long and have not much time to train new men. Nor do the same reasons obtain for a pope to trust the ministers of his predecessor. And since the ministers are men from various countries independent of the papacy, and beneficiaries of things not controlled by the pope and his successors, they neither fear the new pope nor have any hope of continuing in his service. Thus, they are apt to be less devoted and less faithful in his service than those who serve a secular prince.

*   *   *

4. If PRINCES take little account of their servants and scorn them or push them aside for the slightest reason whenever they please, why should a lord be offended or complain when his ministers —provided they do not fall short of their debts of loyalty and honor—leave him or take up with those parties that better serve their interests?

*   *   *

5. If MEN were respectful or grateful enough, it would be the duty of a master to benefit his servants on every occasion, as much as he could. But experience shows—and I have seen this to be the case with my own servants—that as soon as they get their fill, or as soon as the master is unable to treat them as generously as he has in the past, they leave him flat. Thus, to best serve his own interests, a master must be tight-fisted, more readily inclined to be stingy rather than liberal. He must retain their allegiance with hopes rather than deeds. Now, for that to be successful, he must occasionally be very generous to just one of them; and that is enough. For the nature of men is such that hope, as a rule, is stronger than fear. They are more excited and pleased by the sight of one man well rewarded than they are frightened by seeing many men treated poorly.

*   *   *

6. It is a great error to speak of the things of this world absolutely and indiscriminately and to deal with them, as it were, by the book. In nearly all things one must make distinctions and exceptions because of differences in their circumstances. These circumstances are not covered by one and the same rule. Nor can these distinctions and exceptions be found written in books. They must be taught by discretion.

*   *   *

7. UNLESS YOU are forced by necessity, be careful in your conversations never to say anything which, if repeated, might displease others. For often, at times and in ways you could never foresee, those words may do you great harm. In this matter, I warn you, be very careful. Even prudent men go wrong here, and it is difficult not to. But if the difficulty is great, so much greater is the reward for him who knows how to do it.

* * *

8. IF EITHER necessity or contempt induces you to speak ill of another, at least be careful to say things that will offend only him. For instance, if you want to insult a particular person, do not speak ill of his country, his family, or his relatives. It is great folly to offend many if you only want to insult one man.

* * *

9. READ THESE *Ricordi* often, and ponder them well. For it is easier to know and understand them than to put them into practice. But this too becomes easier if you grow so accustomed to them that they are always fresh in your memory.

* * *

10. LET NO ONE trust so much in native intelligence that he believes it to be sufficient without the help of experience. No matter what his natural endowments, any man who has been in a position of responsibility will admit that experience attains many things which natural gifts alone could never attain.

* * *

11. DO NOT let the ingratitude of many men deter you from doing good to others. To do good without ulterior motive is a generous and almost divine thing in itself. Moreover, while doing good, you may come across someone so grateful that he makes up for all the ingratitude of others.

* * *

12. IN EVERY nation, we find nearly all the same or similar proverbs, expressed in different words. The reason is that these

proverbs are born of experience, or observation of things; and
that is the same, or at least similar, everywhere.

* * *

13. IF YOU want to know what the thoughts of tyrants are, read
in Cornelius Tacitus the last conversations of the dying Augustus with Tiberius.

* * *

14. NOTHING IS more precious than friends; therefore, lose no
opportunity to make them. Men will always get together to talk;
and friends can help, and enemies can harm you, in times and
places you would never have expected.

* * *

15. LIKE ALL MEN, I have pursued honor and profit. And often,
I got more than I had wished or hoped. But I never found in
them the satisfaction I had anticipated. A powerful reason, if it
be well considered, for men to lessen their vain cupidity.

* * *

16. POWER AND POSITION are generally sought, because everything
that is beautiful and good about them appears externally, em-
blazoned on their superficies. But the bother, the toil, the troubles, and the dangers lie hidden and unseen. If these were as
obvious as the good things, there would be no reason to seek
power and position, except one: the more men are honored,
revered, and adored, the more they seem to approach and become similar to God. And what man would not want to resemble Him?

* * *

17. DO NOT believe those who say they have voluntarily relin-
quished power and position for love of peace and quiet. Nearly
always, their reason was either levity or necessity. Experience
shows that, as soon as they are offered a chance to return to the
former life, they leave behind their much vaunted peace and
quiet, and seize it with the same fury that fire seizes dry or
oily things.

* * *

18. CORNELIUS TACITUS teaches those who live under tyrants how to live and act prudently; just as he teaches tyrants ways to secure their tyranny.

* * *

19. CONSPIRACIES CANNOT be hatched without the complicity of others, and for that reason they are extremely dangerous. For most men are either stupid or evil, and to take up with such people involves too great a risk.

* * *

20. NOTHING WORKS against the success of a conspiracy so much as the wish to make it ironclad and almost certain to succeed. Such an attempt always requires many men, much time, and very favorable circumstances. And all these in turn heighten the risk of being discovered. You see, therefore, how dangerous conspiracies are! All these factors that would add security to any other enterprise add danger to this one. I think the reason may be that Fortune, who plays such a large role in all matters, becomes angry with those who try to limit her dominion.

* * *

21. ON SEVERAL occasions, I have said and written that the Medici lost control of the state in '27 because they respected so many republican institutions; and that I was afraid the people would lose their liberty because they exercised such tight control of the state.[3] The reasoning behind these two conclusions is this: the Medici regime, being odious to most of the citizens, needed solid support among devoted partisans if it was to maintain itself. These would have had to be men who not only stood to gain a great deal from the government, but who also recognized that they would be ruined and could not remain in Florence if the Medici were expelled. But such supporters were hard to find! For the Medici, trying hard to seem fair to everyone and not wishing to show any partiality towards friends and relatives, were in the habit of distributing

3 The phrases G. uses are *uso di libertà* and *uso di stato*, which I have translated as "republican institutions" and "tight control of the state," thus losing the neat contrast provided by the Italian.

the highest as well as the lower offices widely and generously.

If the Medici had done the contrary, they would certainly be worthy of censure. But even so, they did not gain many adherents to their regime. For although the majority of people were satisfied with the way the Medici conducted themselves, they were not completely won over. The desire to return to the Grand Council [4] was so rooted in the hearts of men that it could not be eradicated by any acts of kindness, mildness, or favor. The friends of the Medici liked the regime, but were not so attached as to run any risk for it. In case of a crisis, they hoped that, by behaving well, they could save themselves as they had done in '94; and thus they were disposed to let things take their course rather than try to withstand an onslaught.[5]

A popular government must take a completely opposite course from the one that would have been favorable to the Medici. Generally, the people of Florence love popular government. It is not a machine guided by one or by a few toward a definite end, but rather changes its direction every day because of the number and the ignorance of those who run it. And therefore, a popular government must keep the favor of the people if it wishes to maintain itself. It must do all it can to stay out of the quarrels among its citizens lest they, having no other recourse, open the way to revolution.[6] In short, popular government must tread the path of justice and equality. From these

[4] The Grand Council was introduced in 1494, after the Medici had been expelled. Citizens were eligible if they were twenty-nine years old, had paid their taxes (*netti di specchio*), and were *beneficiati*, which meant that either their father, grandfather, or great-grandfather had occupied a seat in one of the three highest offices in the government. The Grand Council elected from within itself a council of eighty that functioned as a Senate. It also created the chief magistrates and approved all laws. Of a population of some 55,000, only a few more than three thousand Florentines were eligible for the Grand Council. If the Florentine constitution of 1494 was far more democratic than the Venetian one on which it was modelled, it was certainly not democratic in the modern sense.

[5] After the expulsion of the Medici, few of their supporters and friends suffered any harm, partly because of Savonarola's restraining influence over those who would gladly have done it.

[6] The word *mutazione*, here translated as revolution, means a forced change in government but not necessarily brought about by rebellion and arms. "Change" seemed too weak to convey the meaning of the notion.

are born the security of all and, as a rule, general satisfaction. More, they will provide the basis for preserving popular government—not through a few partisans, which it could not tolerate, but through numerous friends. To continue tight control of the state is impossible, for it transforms popular government into another kind. And that does not preserve liberty but destroys it.

* * *

22. How OFTEN is it said: if only this had been done, that would have happened; or, if only that had not been done, this would not have happened. And yet, if it were possible to test such statements, we should see how false they are.

* * *

23. THE FUTURE is so deceptive and subject to so many accidents, that very often even the wisest of men is fooled when he tries to predict it. If you look very closely at his prognostications, especially when they concern details—for often the general outcome is easier to guess—you will see little difference between them and the guesses of those who are considered less wise. Therefore, to give up a present good for fear of a future evil is, most of the time, madness—unless the evil is very certain, very near, or very great compared to the good. Otherwise, quite often a groundless fear will cause you to lose a good thing you could have kept.

* * *

24. NOTHING IS more fleeting than the memory of benefits received. Therefore, rely more on those whose circumstances do not permit them to fail you than on those whom you have favored. For often they will not remember the favors, or they will suppose them to have been smaller than they were, or they will even claim that you did them almost because you were obliged.

* * *

25. BE CAREFUL not to do anyone the sort of favor that cannot be done without at the same time displeasing others. For injured

men do not forget offenses; in fact, they exaggerate them. Whereas the favored party will either forget or will deem the favor smaller than it was. Therefore, other things being equal, you lose a great deal more than you gain.

*   *   *

26. MEN OUGHT to pay a great deal more attention to substance and realities than to ceremonies. And yet it is incredible how easily people fall for kind, soft words. The reason is that everyone thinks he merits being highly esteemed, and therefore will be indignant if he thinks you are mindless of what he is sure he deserves.

*   *   *

27. IF YOU have doubts about someone, your true and best security consists in having things so arranged that he cannot hurt you even if he wants to. For any security founded on the will and discretion of others is worthless, seeing how little goodness and faith is to be found in men.

*   *   *

28. I KNOW of no one who loathes the ambition, the avarice, and the sensuality of the clergy more than I—both because each of these vices is hateful in itself and because each and all are hardly suited to those who profess to live a life dependent upon God. Furthermore, they are such contradictory vices that they cannot coexist in a subject unless he be very unusual indeed.

In spite of all this, the positions I have held under several popes have forced me, for my own good, to further their interests. Were it not for that, I should have loved Martin Luther as much as myself—not so that I might be free of the laws based on Christian religion as it is generally interpreted and understood; but to see this bunch of rascals get their just deserts, that is, to be either without vices or without authority.

*   *   *

29. I HAVE SAID many times, and it is very true, that it was harder for the Florentines to achieve their small dominion than

for the Venetians to achieve their large territorial gains. For
the Florentines are in a region that knew many liberties, and
these are very hard to extinguish. These provinces are very
hard to conquer and, once conquered, are no less hard to keep.
Besides, the Florentines have the Church nearby, which is
strong and immortal. Though it sometimes seems to stagger,
in the end it reaffirms its rights more strongly than ever. The
Venetians have conquered lands accustomed to servitude, stubborn neither in defense nor in rebellion. And as neighbors they
have had secular princes, whose lives and memories are not
everlasting.

* * *

30. IF YOU consider the matter carefully, you cannot deny that
Fortune has great power over human affairs. We see these affairs
constantly being affected by fortuitous circumstances that men
could neither foresee nor avoid. Although cleverness and care
may accomplish many things, they are nevertheless not enough.
Man also needs good Fortune.

* * *

31. EVEN IF YOU attribute everything to prudence and virtue
and discount as much as possible the power of Fortune, you
must at least admit that it is very important to be born or
to live in a time that prizes highly the virtues and qualities
in which you excel. Take the example of Fabius Maximus,
whose great reputation resulted from his being by nature hesi-
tant. He found himself in a war in which impetuosity was
ruinous, whereas procrastination was useful. At another time,
the opposite could have been true. His times needed his qualities, and that was his fortune. To be sure, if a man could change
his nature to suit the conditions of the times, he would be much
less dominated by Fortune. But that is most difficult, and perhaps even impossible.

* * *

32. AMBITION IS NOT a reprehensible quality, nor are ambitious
men to be censured, if they seek glory through honorable and

honest means. In fact, it is they who produce great and excellent works. Those who lack this passion are cold spirits, inclined more toward laziness than activity. But ambition is pernicious and detestable when it has as its sole end power, as is generally the case with princes. And when they make it their goal, they will level conscience, honor, humanity, and everything else to attain it.

* * *

33. THE PROVERB tells us that a dishonestly acquired fortune is never enjoyed by an heir of the third generation. If this were so because such wealth is contaminated, it would seem that the man who acquired it ought to enjoy it least of all. The reason he is allowed to enjoy it was once told me by my father. According to Saint Augustine, no one is so wicked that he does not do some good. God, who leaves no good unrewarded and no evil unpunished, gives such a man enjoyment in this world as remuneration for his good deeds, only to punish him fully in the next for his evil deeds. But since ill-gotten gains had to be purged, they could not pass to a third heir. I answered that I did not know whether the proverb itself was true, since one could cite many experiences to the contrary. But if it were true, there might be another reason for it. The natural vicissitude of human affairs brings poverty where there once were riches. And this is more true for heirs than it is for the founder of the fortune. For the more time passes, the more easily do changes come about. Furthermore, the founder, the man who acquired the fortune, is more attached to it. Just as he knew how to acquire it, so he also knows the art of keeping it intact. And being used to living frugally, he does not squander it. But heirs do not have the same attachment to a fortune they have come by effortlessly. They have been reared in wealth but have not learned the art of earning it. Who can wonder, then, that they let it slip through their fingers, either through waste or carelessness?

* * *

34. ALL THINGS whose end comes about not through violence but through gradual wearing away have a much longer life than you would at first suppose. We can see this in the example

of a consumptive who is judged to be at his end but who lives on, not just for days, but for weeks and months. So, too, in a city that must be taken by siege, provisions last much longer than anyone would have thought.

* * *

35. How DIFFERENT theory is from practice! So many people understand things well but either do not remember or do not know how to put them into practice! The knowledge of such men is useless. It is like having a treasure stored in a chest without ever being able to take it out.

* * *

36. IF YOU are seeking the favor of men, be careful never to give a flat refusal to anyone who makes a request of you. Rather you should give evasive answers, for it may happen that someone who asked for something will not need it later. Or else circumstances may arise that make your excuses seem convincing. Furthermore, many men are foolish and easily swayed by words. Even without doing what you could not or would not do, you can often leave a person well satisfied by answering him cleverly, whereas if you had refused him outright, he would dislike you no matter how things turned out subsequently.

* * *

37. ALWAYS DENY what you don't want to be known, and always affirm what you want to be believed. For, though there be much—even conclusive—evidence to the contrary, a fervent affirmation or denial will often create at least some doubt in the mind of your listener.

* * *

38. ALTHOUGH THE house of the Medici is powerful and has produced two popes, it is much harder for it to keep control of the Florentine state than it was for Cosimo,[7] a private citizen.

7 Cosimo de' Medici (1389–1464). After a brief exile, Cosimo returned to Florence in 1434, defeated the powerful rival family of the Albizzi, and became the power behind the Florentine government. Though few changes

Aside from his extraordinary ability, Cosimo was aided by the conditions of his times. With the help of only a few men, he was able to take and keep control of the government, without displeasing the many, who did not yet know freedom. Indeed, in his day, the middle and lowest classes were able to better their conditions every time the strong quarreled, and every time a revolution took place.

Now that the people have had a taste of the Grand Council, however, it is no longer a matter of seizing or usurping power from the hands of four, six, ten, or twenty citizens, but from the entire people. And they are so attached to their liberty that there is no chance of having them forget it—not with all the kindness, with all the good government, or with all the recognition and exaltation of the people that the Medici or any other powers may attempt.

* * *

39. Our father had children of such excellent qualities that, in his day, he was considered the most fortunate parent in Florence. Even so, I have often thought that, all things considered, we were more trouble to him than we were solace. Think what must be the plight of those whose children are crazy, evil, or unfortunate.

* * *

40. It is a great thing to have authority. If you use it well, men will fear you even more than your powers warrant. Not knowing exactly the extent of your authority, they will quickly decide to yield rather than contest whether you can do what you threaten.

* * *

41. If men were wise and good, those in authority should certainly be gentle rather than severe with them. But since the

---

were made in the organization of the state, Cosimo dominated elections and voting lists, kept the favor of the public, and made other powerful families come to depend upon him. He enjoyed uncontested dominion until his death in 1464, when the city conferred upon him the title *Pater Patriae*.

majority of men are either not very good or not very wise, one must rely more on severity than on kindness. Whoever thinks otherwise is mistaken. Surely, anyone who can skillfully mix and blend the one with the other would produce the sweetest possible accord and harmony. But heaven endows few with such talents; perhaps no one.

* * *

42. DO NOT strive harder to gain favor than to keep your good reputation. When you lose your good reputation, you also lose good will, which is replaced by contempt. But the man who maintains his reputation will never lack friends, favor, and good will.

* * *

43. IN MY various administrative posts I have observed that when I wanted to bring about peace, civil accord, and the like, it was better, before stepping in, to let matters be debated thoroughly and for a long time. In the end, out of weariness, both sides would beg me to reconcile them. Thus, at their invitation, with good reputation, and without a single note of cupidity, I could accomplish what seemed impossible at first.

* * *

44. DO ALL you can to seem good, for that can be infinitely useful. But since false opinions do not last, it will be difficult to seem good for very long, if you are really not. My father once told me this.

* * *

45. HE ALSO used to say, in praise of thrift, that a ducat in your purse does you more credit than ten you have spent.

* * *

46. IN MY administrations I never liked cruelty or excessive punishments. Nor are they necessary. Except for certain cases that must serve as example, you can sufficiently maintain fear if you punish crimes with three quarters of the penalty, provided you make it a rule to punish all crimes.

47. LEARNING IMPOSED on weak minds does not improve them, and it may ruin them. But when it is added to natural talent, it makes men perfect and almost divine.

* * *

48. POLITICAL POWER cannot be wielded according to the dictates of good conscience. If you consider its origin, you will always find it in violence—except in the case of republics within their territories, but not beyond. Not even the emperor is exempt from this rule; nor are the priests, whose violence is double, since they assault us with both temporal and spiritual arms.

* * *

49. TELL NO ONE anything you want kept secret, for there are many things that move men to gossip. Some do it through foolishness, some for profit, others through vanity, to seem in the know. And if you unnecessarily told your secret to another, you need not be surprised if he does the same, since it matters less to him than to you that it be known.

* * *

50. WASTE NO TIME with revolutions that do not remove the causes of your complaints but that simply change the faces of those in charge. For you will still remain dissatisfied. To take an example: what good does it do to rid the Medici of Ser Giovanni da Poppi, if he is replaced by ser Bernardino da San Miniato,[8] a man of the same quality and calibre?

* * *

51. IN FLORENCE, anyone who tries to overthrow the regime is very unwise, unless he do it out of necessity, or because he hopes to be head of the new government. For if the attempt should fail, he has endangered himself and all his possessions. And if it succeeds, he will gain only a fraction of what he had

---

8 Ser Giovanni da Poppi was secretary to Lorenzo, duke of Urbino; Bernardino da San Miniato was Lorenzo's military chargé d'affaires in Genoa. Both men were, apparently, universally disliked.

envisaged. What folly it is to play a game in which you can lose incomparably more than you can win. And what matters perhaps even more, once you have brought about your revolution, you will face a constant torment: the fear of a new revolution.

* * *

52. WE SEE from experience that nearly everyone who has helped another to attain power will, as time passes, enjoy small returns for his efforts. The reason is said to be that, knowing the man's ability, the prince fears he may some day try to take back what he has given. But it may also come about because the man, believing his services to have been great, wants more than his due. That not being forthcoming, he becomes malcontent, and from that are born anger and suspicion between him and the prince.

* * *

53. EACH TIME that you, who have caused or helped me to become prince, want me to govern as you say, or want me to concede to you things that diminish my authority, you are cancelling the good you have done me. For you are seeking, partly or completely, to deprive me of what you helped me to acquire.

* * *

54. ANYONE CHARGED with defending a land must make it his principal object to hold out as long as possible. For, as the proverb says, he who has time has life. Delay brings infinite opportunities that at first could not be known or hoped for.

* * *

55. DO NOT spend now, relying on future profits, for they very often do not come or are smaller than expected. Whereas, on the contrary, expenses always multiply. It is this miscalculation that causes so many merchants to go bankrupt. They take out notes in order to use the cash to make larger profits. But when these do not materialize or are slow in coming, they run the risk of being overwhelmed by their notes, which never

cease and never diminish but always continue to run and to devour.

*　*　*

56. WISE ECONOMY consists not so much in avoiding spending—for that is often necessary—as in knowing how to spend well; that is, to spend a grosso, and get twenty-four quattrini's worth.[9]

*　*　*

57. How MUCH luckier astrologers are than other men! By telling one truth among a hundred lies, they acquire the confidence of men, and their falsehoods are believed. Other men, by telling one lie among many true statements, lose the confidence of others, and no one believes them even when they speak the truth. This comes about because of the curiosity of men. Desirous of knowing the future, and having no other way to do it, they go running after anyone who promises to reveal it to them.

*　*　*

58. How WISELY the philosopher spoke when he said: "Of future contingencies there can be no determined truth". Go where you will: the farther you go, the more you will find this saying to be absolutely true.

*　*　*

59. I ONCE said to Pope Clement,[10] who was frightened by the slightest danger, that a good cure for this baseless fear was to remember how often he had been frightened needlessly by similar circumstances. I do not give this advice to make men stop fearing altogether, but only to get them used to not being always afraid.

*　*　*

60. A SUPERIOR intellect is bestowed upon men only to make them unhappy and tormented. For it does nothing but produce

---

[9] That is, to get double your money's worth.

[10] Pope (1523–34) Clement VII was Giulio de' Medici, son of Giuliano and nephew of Lorenzo the Magnificent. He was a shrewd but timid and vacillating pope, as G. often points out.

in them greater turmoil and anxiety than there is in more limited men.

* * *

61. MEN HAVE different temperaments. Some are so full of hope that they count as certain what they do not yet have; others are so fearful that they do not count on anything not yet in their hands. I am closer to the second than the first. And men of my temperament will be less often deceived but will live with greater torment.

* * *

62. PEOPLE GENERALLY—and inexperienced men always—are more easily moved by the hope of gain than by the danger of loss. And yet the contrary should be true, for the desire to keep is more natural than the desire to gain. The reason for the mistake is that, ordinarily, hope is stronger than fear. Men easily allay their fears, even when they are warranted; and hope, even when there is no hope.

* * *

63. WE SEE that the old are more avaricious than the young. And yet the contrary should be true, for, having less time to live, they need less. The reason is said to be that the old are more timorous. But I don't believe it, for I see many of them who are more cruel, more lecherous—in thought if not in deed —and more afraid of death than the young. The reason, I believe, is that the longer a man lives, the more does he become accustomed to and fond of the things of this world. Thus, the old are more strongly attached to those things, and more easily moved by them.

* * *

64. BEFORE 1494, wars were long, campaigns were relatively bloodless, and methods of conquest were slow and difficult. And although artillery was already in use, it was handled so unskillfully that it did little damage. Thus, those who held power stood in little danger of losing it. When the French came to Italy, they introduced such efficiency into war that,

up to 1521, the loss of a campaign meant the loss of a state. The first to teach us how to withstand the onslaught of armies was Signor Prospero, with his defense of Milan.[11] Through that example, rulers now have the same security they had before 1494 but for a different reason. Then, it was due to the fact that men were unskilled in the art of offense; now, to the fact of knowing well the art of defense.

* * *

65. THE FIRST man to call the baggage of an army "impedimenta" could not have found a better name. And whoever coined the phrase that says something "is more trouble than moving a camp," was very right. It is an endless task to get everything in a camp organized so that it can move.

* * *

66. DON'T BELIEVE those who so fervently preach liberty. Nearly all of them—probably every single one of them—has his own particular interests in mind. Experience proves beyond any doubt that if they thought they would be better off under an absolute government, they would rush into it as fast as they could.

* * *

67. NO OFFICE or position in the world requires more ability than the command of an army. This is true not only because of the importance of the position itself, but also because the captain must think about and settle an infinite variety of matters. He must be able to foresee things from afar, and to repair damage immediately.

* * *

[11] G. is referring to the invasion of Italy by Charles VIII of France in 1494 and to the fact that in the initial stages French arms carried everything before them. In a later phase of the Italian Wars, which were mainly a contest between Charles V and Francis I, Prospero Colonna, in the Imperial service, successfully defended Milan against an attack by French and Swiss forces. G. is referring o Colonna's defensive stand at a villa a few miles outside Milan. The engagement was known as the Battle of La Bicocca (April 27, 1522).

68. To BE NEUTRAL when others are at war is a wise course for the strong, who need not fear the victor. For the strong man can maintain himself without trouble, and he can hope to gain from the disorders of the others. In any other case, neutrality is ill-considered and harmful, for the neutral party remains the prey of both victor and vanquished. Worst of all is neutrality born, not of judgment, but of irresolution. For example: being unable to reach a decision, you conduct yourself in a way that does not satisfy even those who, for the time being, would be content with an assurance of neutrality. This mistake is committed more often by republics than by princes, because it is often caused by divisions among those who must make decisions. One advises this, the other that, and there are never enough who agree to make one opinion prevail over the other. That is exactly what happened in 1512.[12]

*　　*　　*

69. If you observe well, you will see that, from one age to another, there is a change not only in men's speech, vocabulary, dress, style of building, culture, and such things, but, what is more, even in their sense of taste. A food that was highly prized in one age will often be found far less appetizing in another.

*　　*　　*

70. The true test of a man's spirit comes when he is visited by an unexpected danger. Those who hold out—and they are few—may truly be called brave and dauntless.

*　　*　　*

71. If you see a city beginning to decline, a government changing, a new empire expanding, or any such phenomenon—and

[12] The Florentines refused to join the Holy League (cf. n. 1 in Series B), but gave little assistance to the French, trying to pursue a policy of feeble neutrality. When the French were driven back toward the Alps despite their signal victory at Ravenna, the Florentines became prey to the Spanish army and the pope. Cardinal Giovanni de' Medici (the future Pope Leo X) returned to Florence, the Medici were restored, and the constitution of 1494 was undone.

these things are sometimes quite clearly visible to us—be careful not to misjudge the time they will take. By their very nature, and because of various obstacles, such movements are much slower than most men imagine. And to be mistaken in these matters can be very harmful to you. Be very careful, for it is a step on which people often stumble. The same is true even of private and personal affairs; but much more so of public and general matters, for these, because of their bulk, move much more slowly and are subject to many more accidents.

*   *   *

72. THERE IS nothing in life more desirable or more glorious than to see your enemy prostrate on the ground and at your mercy. And this glory is doubled if you use it well, that is, by showing mercy and being content to have won.

*   *   *

73. NEITHER ALEXANDER THE GREAT, nor Caesar, nor anyone else famous for his clemency, ever exercised it when he knew it would endanger the fruits of his victory. That, indeed, would have been folly. They showed mercy only when it did not diminish their security and when it added to their fame.

*   *   *

74. REVENGE DOES not always stem from hate or from an evil nature. Sometimes it is necessary so that people will learn not to offend you. It is perfectly all right to avenge yourself even though you feel no deep rancor against the person who is the object of your revenge.

*   *   *

75. POPE LEO used to cite his father, Lorenzo de' Medici, who often said: "Remember that those who speak ill of us don't love us."

*   *   *

76. EVERYTHING THAT has been in the past and is in the present will be in the future. But the names and appearances of things change, so that he who has not a discerning eye will not

recognize them. Nor will he know what line to take or what judgment to form.

* * *

77. WHEN I was ambassador to Spain, I observed that whenever His Catholic Majesty Ferdinand of Aragon,[13] most powerful and wise prince, was about to embark on some new enterprise, or make a decision of great importance, he went about it in such a way that before his intentions were known, the whole court and the people were already insisting and exclaiming: the king must do such and so. Then we would announce his decision just when all hoped and clamored for it, and it is incredible what justification and favor it found among his subjects and in his dominions.

* * *

78. IF YOU attempt certain things at the right time, they are easy to accomplish—in fact, they almost get done by themselves. If you undertake them before the time is right, not only will they fail, but they will often become impossible to accomplish even when the time would have been right. Therefore, do not rush things madly, do not precipitate them; wait for them to mature, wait for the right season.

* * *

79. UNLESS RIGHTLY understood, it would be a dangerous proverb that enjoins the wise man to take advantage of the benefits brought by time. For opportunity knocks at your door just once, and in many cases you have to decide and to act quickly. But when you are in difficult straits or involved in troublesome affairs, procrastinate, and wait as long as you can. For often time will enlighten or free you. Using the proverb thus, it is always salutary. But understood differently, it could be harmful.

* * *

80. LUCKY ARE THOSE to whom the same opportunity returns more than once. For even a wise man may miss it or misuse

---

13 Ferdinand V of Aragon (1452–1516), known as Ferdinand the Catholic. G. was Florentine ambassador to his court for two years (1512–14).

it the first time. But not to recognize or use it the second
time is to be very foolish indeed.

* * *

81. ALTHOUGH A future event may seem inevitable, do not depend upon it completely. Provided you can do so without
upsetting everything, you should have alternate plans, in case
the opposite of what you expect should occur. Experience
shows this to be the wise course to take, for things quite often
turn out very differently from what had been generally pre-
dicted.

* * *

82. SMALL BEGINNINGS, hardly worthy of notice, are often the
cause of great misfortune or of great success. Thus, it is very
wise to note and to weigh everything, no matter how tiny.

* * *

83. I USED TO think that what did not occur to me at once
would not occur to me later, no matter how much I thought
about it. But in fact, as I have seen in my own case and with
others, the opposite is true. The more and the better one thinks
about things, the better they are understood and carried out.

* * *

84. IF YOU want to be a man of affairs, don't let any deal slip
through your fingers, for you will not easily get it back when
you want. Whereas if you are continually running things, one
deal will follow the other, without your having to use diligence
or industry to get them.

* * *

85. FORTUNE VARIES not only among men but even in the same
man. You may be fortunate in one enterprise and unfortunate
in another. I have been successful in those gains that are made
without capital, applying only personal industry; in others,
I have been unsuccessful. Things were hard to get when I
sought them; when I was not looking for them, they came
running after me.

* * *

86. If you are involved in important affairs or are seeking power, you must always hide your failures and exaggerate your successes. It is a form of swindling and very much against my nature. But, since your fate more often depends upon the opinion of others rather than on facts, it is a good idea to create the impression that things are going well. The opposite reputation will be harmful to you.

* * *

87. From your relatives and friends you receive many favors of which neither you nor they are aware; indeed, these far outnumber the favors that are known to come from them. For rarely do things happen that require your requesting their aid, whereas, in the course of daily life, you will profit just from the fact that it is believed you can use them whenever you need.

* * *

88. A prince, or indeed anyone involved in important affairs, ought not only to keep those things secret which it is better were not known, but must also accustom himself and his ministers to be silent about all things—even seemingly insignificant and unimportant matters—with the exception of those which it is advantageous to broadcast. If your subjects and those around you know nothing of your affairs, they will always be in suspense, almost in wonderment, and will pay heed to your every move and step.

* * *

89. Unless my source is unimpeachable, I am loath to believe any news that seems probable. Since men are predisposed to believe such news, it is easy to find those who will invent it; whereas the improbable or the unexpected will not be so easily made up. Therefore, when I hear expected news from an unreliable source, I am more skeptical than when I hear unexpected news.

* * *

90. Men dependent upon the favor of a prince are attentive to his every gesture, his slightest sign, so that they may jump

to serve him at his pleasure. And this often causes them grave harm. One should keep a level head, not be overanxious, and make a move only when the matter is important enough to warrant it.

* * *

91. I COULD never get it into my head that God's justice would allow the state of Milan to be enjoyed by the children of Ludovico Sforza, who acquired it so wickedly, and to acquire it, ruined the whole world.[14]

* * *

92. NEVER SAY "God helped so and so because he is good, and that so and so was unsuccessful because he is evil." For we often see that the opposite is true. But neither must we say God is not just. His ways are so past finding out, that they are rightly called *abyssus multa*.[15]

* * *

93. A PRIVATE citizen can wrong his prince and commit *crimen lese maiestatis* by doing that which properly belongs to the prince; but likewise, a prince may commit *crimen lese populi* by doing that which properly belongs to the people and to private citizens. Thus, the duke of Ferrara is very reprehensible indeed, for he indulges in commerce, monopolies, and other vulgar things that ought to be done by private citizens.[16]

* * *

[14] Gian Galeazzo, a minor, became duke under the regency of his mother, Bona of Savoy. Simonetta, who had been secretary to the young duke's father Galeazzo and to his grandfather Francesco before him, actually managed the affairs of government. Ludovico Sforza (il Moro), brother of Galeazzo, usurped power from Bona, had Simonetta killed (1480), and took over the reins of government. Gian Galeazzo married Isabella of Naples, daughter of the powerful duke of Calabria. When this duke seemed intent on restoring his son-in-law's rights in Milan, Ludovico allied himself with Charles VIII of France, who came to Italy, and thus began the series of devastating Italian wars to which G. is referring.

[15] *Rom.* 11 : 33. G. seldom cites the Bible.

[16] Duke Alfonso I of Ferrara. An excellent mechanic, whose cannon were famous throughout Europe.

94. IF YOU frequent the court of a prince, hoping to be employed by him, keep yourself constantly in view. For often, matters will arise suddenly; and if you are in sight, he will remember you and commit them to your trust, whereas if you are not, he might entrust them to another.

* * *

95. THE MAN who confronts dangers thoughtlessly, without recognizing them, is bestial; he who recognizes dangers but does not fear more than necessary, is brave.

* * *

96. IT IS an old saying that all wise men are timid, because they know all the dangers and therefore have cause to be afraid. I think this saying is wrong. Anyone who judges a danger to be greater than it is ought not to be called a wise man. I would call wise the man who knows the extent of a danger and fears it only as much as he should. A brave man, then, ought sooner to be called wise than a timid man. Assuming that both see matters clearly, the difference between them lies in that the timid man takes into account all the dangers he recognizes, and supposes the worst; whereas the brave man, though he too recognizes them all, considers that some can be avoided by human industry and that some will disappear by chance. He will not let himself be abashed by them all, but will embark on his course with the knowledge and hope that not everything that can happen need happen.

* * *

97. WHEN CLEMENT was made pope, the marquis of Pescara [17] said to me that this was perhaps the only time he had ever seen something happen which was universally desired. The reason for this could be that generally it is the few, not the many,

[17] The marquis of Pescara (Ferrante Francesco D'Avalos), an Imperial general, was chiefly responsible for the great victory over the French at the Battle of Pavia (1525). When Morone, a partisan of the dispossessed Sforzas, tried to get him to join their cause in the interests of Italy against the foreigners, Pescara revealed he plot to the emperor. His character and intentions have been the subject of controversy ever since.

who determine the affairs of the world. And since the aims of the few are almost always different from those of the many, they give birth to effects different from those desired by the many.

*   *   *

98. ALTHOUGH A prudent tyrant will look with favor on timid wise men, he will also not be displeased by brave ones, if he knows them to be of quiet temperament, for he can always hope to satisfy them. It is the brave and restless men that he dislikes above all, because he cannot assume he will be able to satisfy them. And therefore he is forced to think about extinguishing them.

*   *   *

99. UNLESS THE prudent tyrant consider me an enemy, I would rather he thought me restless and brave than timid. For he will try to satisfy me, whereas with the other sort, he will do as he pleases.[18]

*   *   *

100. IF YOU live under a tyrant, it is better to be his friend only to a certain extent rather than be completely intimate with him. In this way, if you are a respected citizen, you will profit from his power—sometimes even more than do those closer to him. And if he should fall, you may still hope to save yourself.

*   *   *

101. THERE IS no rule or prescription for saving yourself from a bestial and cruel tyrant, except the one that applies for the plague. Run as far and as fast as you can.

*   *   *

102. ANYONE WHO is besieged and is expecting help will always proclaim his need to be greater than it is. But someone who

18 This *ricordo* obviously contradicts the preceding one. Spongano thinks it may have been simply a mistake, and that G., in a movement of distraction, let *inquieto* (restless) pass for *quieto* (quiet). It is hard to think otherwise.

does not expect help, having no alternative but to tire the enemy and make him lose hope, will hide his needs and minimize them publicly.

*   *   *

103. A TYRANT will do everything possible to discover your secret thoughts. He will be affectionate, will talk to you at great length, will have you observed by men he has ordered to become intimate with you. It is difficult to guard yourself against all these snares. If you do not want him to know, think carefully, and guard yourself with consummate industry against anything that might give you away, using as much diligence to hide your secret thoughts as he uses to discover them.

*   *   *

104. MEN WHO are of an open and genuine nature and, as they say in Florence, "frank," are very praiseworthy and pleasing to everyone. Deception, on the other hand, is odious and disliked. But deception is very useful, whereas your frankness tends to profit others rather than you. Still, since it cannot be denied that deception is not a pleasant thing, I would praise the man who is ordinarily open and frank and who uses deception only in very rare, important matters. Thus, you will have the reputation of being open and genuine, and you will enjoy the popularity such reputation brings. And in those very important matters, you will reap even greater advantage from deception, because your reputation for not being a deceiver will make your words be easily believed.

*   *   *

105. EVEN THOUGH a man be a known dissimulator and deceiver, his deceptions will nevertheless, on occasion, find believers. It seems strange, but it is very true. I remember that His Catholic Majesty, more than any other man, had such a reputation; and yet there was never any lack of people who believed him more than they should. This stems necessarily either from the simplicity or from the greed of men. The

latter believe too easily what they wish were true; the former simply do not know what is happening.

* * *

106. NOTHING IN our civic life is more difficult than marrying off our daughters well. The reason is that all men think more of themselves than others do, and thus they begin to reach for heights which in fact they cannot attain. I have seen many fathers refuse matches which, after they had looked around, they would have accepted gratefully. Men should, therefore, measure accurately their own condition as well as that of others, and not be led astray by a higher opinion of themselves than is warranted. I know all this well, though I do not know whether I shall use the knowledge well. Nor do I know whether I shall fall into the common error of presuming more than I should. But neither ought this *ricordo* serve to disgust anyone so much that, like Francesco Vettori,[19] he give his daughters to the first man who asks for them.

* * *

107. BEST OF all is not to be born a subject.[20] But if it must be, then it is better to be the subject of a prince than of a republic. For a republic represses all its subjects and gives only its own citizens a share of power. A prince acts more equably towards all; the one is as much his subject as the other. Thus, everyone may hope to receive benefits and employment from him.

* * *

108. NO MAN is so wise that he does not occasionally make a mistake. Good fortune consists in making minor mistakes, or in making them in matters of small consequence.

* * *

[19] Francesco Vettori (1474–1539), Florentine diplomat and statesman, and intimate friend of G. and Machiavelli. His principal work was the *Storia d'Italia dal 1511 al 1527*, but he is far better known for his correspondence with Machiavelli.
[20] By "subject" G. means here someone born in a state dominated by or dependent upon another state.

109. THE FRUIT of liberties and the end for which they were instituted is not government by everyone—for only the able and deserving should govern—but the observance of just laws and order, both of which are more secure in a republic than under the rule of one or few. And therein lies the difficulty that so troubles our city. Men are not satisfied to be free and secure: they also want to govern.

* * *

110. HOW WRONG it is to cite the Romans at every turn. For any comparison to be valid, it would be necessary to have a city with conditions like theirs, and then to govern it according to their example. In the case of a city with different qualities, the comparison is as much out of order as it would be to expect a jackass to race like a horse.[21]

* * *

111. COMMON MEN find the variety of opinions that exists among lawyers quite reprehensible, without realizing that it proceeds not from any defect in the men but from the nature of the subject. General rules cannot possibly comprehend all particular cases. Often, specific cases cannot be decided on the basis of law, but must rather be dealt with by the opinions of men, which are not always in harmony. We see the same thing happen with doctors, philosophers, commercial arbitrators, and in the discourses of those who govern the state, among whom there is no less variety of judgment than among lawyers.

* * *

112. MESSER ANTONIO DA VENAFRA used to say very rightly, "Put six or eight wise men together, and they become so many madmen." The reason is that whenever they disagree on any matter, they would rather argue than resolve it.

* * *

113. IT IS a mistake to think that the law subjects any matter to the arbitrary judgment—that is, to the free will—of the

[21] This *ricordo* seems to be aimed directly at Machiavelli.

judge. For the law never gives the judge power to give or to take away. But those cases which the law cannot determine by a fixed rule must be left to the discretion of the judge. After considering all the circumstances and ramifications of the case, he must determine what he thinks is right, according to his synteresis and his conscience. And in such cases, the judge need answer to no man for his decisions; but he must answer to God, who knows whether he has decided justly.

* * *

114. SOME MEN write discourses on the future, basing themselves on current events. And if they are informed men, their writings will seem very plausible to the reader. Nevertheless, they are completely misleading. For since one conclusion depends upon the other, if one is wrong, all that are deduced from it will be mistaken. But every tiny, particular circumstance that changes is apt to alter a conclusion. The affairs of this world, therefore, cannot be judged from afar but must be judged and resolved day by day.

* * *

115. IN CERTAIN old notebooks written before the year 1457, I find that a wise citizen said: "Either Florence will undo the *Monte,* or the *Monte* will undo Florence." [22] He fully understood that it was necessary for the city to diminish the importance of the *Monte,* else it would grow so much that it would become impossible to control. And yet the conflict has gone on for a long time, without producing the disorder he foresaw. Certainly its development has been much slower than he seems to have anticipated.

* * *

116. A MAN who governs a state must not be frightened by the appearance of dangers, though they seem great, close, and

[22] The *Monte* was the Florentine national debt. The various forms of loans to the state were consolidated in 1347 into a unified national debt, carrying an unalterable interest rate of five percent. When money became scarce, the fixed rate could be, and was, circumvented by registering a loan to the state at twice or even three times the given amount, thus letting it bear ten and fifteen percent interest.

imminent. For, as the proverb says, the devil is not as ugly as he is made out to be. Often dangers will evaporate by chance. And even if something bad should happen, you will always find some remedy or alleviation within the situation itself. Ponder this *ricordo* well, for it is a matter of daily life.

* * *

117. To JUDGE by example is very misleading. Unless they are similar in every respect, examples are useless, since every tiny difference in the case may be a cause of great variations in the effects. And to discern these tiny differences takes a good and perspicacious eye.

* * *

118. A MAN who esteems honor highly will succeed in everything, since he takes no account of toil, danger, or money. I have experienced it myself, and therefore I can say it and write it: the actions of men who do not have this burning stimulus are dead and vain.

* * *

119. DOCUMENTS ARE rarely falsified at the start. It is usually done later, as occasion or necessity dictates. To protect yourself, it is a good idea to have an authentic copy made immediately after the instrument or document is drawn up, and to keep it close by.

* * *

120. THE MAJORITY of crimes that are committed in divided cities originates in suspicion. Doubting each other's good faith, each man decides to act before the other gets him. A man who governs such a city, therefore, must seek first and foremost to remove suspicions.

* * *

121. DO NOT attempt any innovations in the hope that the public will support you, for that is a dangerous foundation. The public may not be of a mind to follow you, and often may

have ideas completely different from what you believe. Look at the example of Brutus and Cassius. After having murdered Caesar, not only did they fail to get the support of the people, as they had expected, but for fear of them were forced to flee to the Capitol.

* * *

122. SEE HOW men deceive themselves. The sins they do not commit they consider ugly; the ones they do commit are venial. Good and evil is often measured by that standard, rather than by considering the nature and the quality of our actions.

* * *

123. QUITE CLEARLY, men in all ages have considered many things to be miracles that were far from being such. But it is certain that every religion has had its own miracles. Thus, miracles are a weak proof of the truth of one faith over another. Perhaps miracles do display the power of God; but no more the God of the Christians than the gods of the Gentiles. Perhaps it would not even be a sin to say that miracles, like prophecies, are secrets of nature, the reasons for which the human intellect cannot fathom.

* * *

124. IN EVERY nation, and in almost every city, I have observed certain devotions intended to produce the same effects. In Florence, Santa Maria Impruneta [23] makes rain and good weather; in other places I have seen virgins and saints do the same—a clear sign that the grace of God succors everyone. Of course, it may also be that these devotions are brought about more by the credulity of men than because anyone really sees their effects.

* * *

125. PHILOSOPHERS AND theologians, and all those who investi-

---

[23] Santa Maria Impruneta is a small town about five miles south of Florence. It is said to have received its name from the ancient sanctuary that contains an image of the Virgin Mary. Since the sanctuary is in the midst of a pine forest, it was called Santa Maria in Pineta, later corrupted to Impruneta. The image is said to have miraculous powers.

gate the supernatural and the invisible, say thousands of insane things. As a matter of fact, men are in the dark about such matters, and their investigation has served and serves more to exercise the intellect than to find truth.

* * *

126. IT WOULD certainly be desirable to do or carry out things perfectly; that is, to have them free of the slightest defect or disorder. But that is very difficult. And so it is a mistake to spend too much time polishing things up, for very often, opportunities will flee while you are losing time trying to make something precisely the way you want it. Indeed, even when you think you have succeeded, you notice later that you were wrong. For the nature of things in this world is such that nearly everything contains some imperfection in all its parts. You must resolve to take things as they are, and to consider good that which has in it the least evil.

* * *

127. DURING THE war, I often witnessed the arrival of news which would have made you think things were going very badly; suddenly other news would arrive that seemed to promise victory. At other times, the good news arrived first, and then the bad. I witnessed these fluctuations very often indeed. In view of this, a good captain should not be easily depressed or elated.

* * *

128. IN AFFAIRS of state, you should guide yourself not so much by what reason demonstrates a prince ought to do as by what he will most likely do, according to his nature or habits. Princes will often do what they please or what they know, and not what they should. If you guide yourself by any rule other than this, you will get into very great trouble.

* * *

129. IF IT were a crime or an injustice to commit a certain act, one cannot say that not committing it would therefore be a good work or a favor. For between offending and favoring, be-

tween a praiseworthy and a blameworthy act, there is a middle ground: and that is to abstain from evil, to abstain from offending. Therefore, do not let men say I did not do this, I did not say that. True merit generally lies in being able to say I did it, I said it.

* * *

130. LET A prince guard himself above all against those who are discontents by nature. No matter how much he favors them or showers them with gifts, he can never be sure of them.

* * *

131. THERE IS a great difference between discontented subjects and desperate subjects. Though the discontents may want to hurt you, they will not run any risks lightly. Rather they will wait for an opportunity, and sometimes it never comes. Desperate men go seeking and soliciting opportunities, and will plunge precipitously into all sorts of revolutionary hopes and schemes. Thus, you need only seldom guard yourself against the discontents, but you must be constantly on your guard against the desperate ones.

* * *

132. I HAVE been of a very easy-going nature, very opposed to bargaining. Men who have had to deal with me have had an easy time of it. Nevertheless, I have learned the most advantageous way to negotiate in all matters: namely, do not reveal immediately the ultimate point to which you would be willing to go. Rather remain distant from it, let yourself be pulled toward it step by step, reluctantly. If you do this, you will often get more than you had expected. But if you deal as I have dealt, you will never get anything but the bare minimum necessary for an agreement.

* * *

133. THOUGH FEW men can do it, it is very wise to hide your displeasure with others, so long as it does you no shame or harm. For it often happens that later you will need the help

of these people, and you can hardly get it if they already know you dislike them. It has happened to me very often that I have had to seek help from someone towards whom I was very ill disposed. And he, believing the contrary, or at least not knowing the truth, served me without hesitation.

* * *

134. ALL MEN are by nature inclined towards good rather than evil. Nor is there anyone who would not rather do good than evil, unless other factors induce him to the contrary. But human nature is so fragile, and temptations are so many, that men let themselves be easily deviated from the good. For that reason, wise legislators invented rewards and punishments, which amount to nothing more than using hope and fear to keep men firm in their natural inclination.

* * *

135. IF THERE is someone naturally more inclined toward evil than good, you may surely say that he is not a man but a beast or a monster, for he is lacking in that inclination which is natural to all men.

* * *

136. IT SOMETIMES happens that fools do greater things than wise men. The reason is that the wise man, unless forced to do otherwise, will rely a great deal on reason and little on fortune; whereas the fool does just the opposite. And things brought about by fortune sometimes have incredible success. The wise men of Florence would have given in to the present storm; the fools, having decided against all the dictates of reason to oppose it, have until now done things which it would have been impossible to believe our city could ever accomplish. That is just what the proverb says: *Audaces fortuna juvat*.[24]

* * *

137. IF THE harmful results of bad government were visible in detail, those who do not know how to govern would either try

[24] "Fortune helps the bold." G. is referring again to the siege of Florence.

to learn or would willingly relinquish the government to able men. But the trouble is that men, and especially the common people, are too ignorant to understand the cause of disorders, and thus do not attribute them to the mistake that brought them about. Not recognizing how much harm is caused by unskilled leaders, they persevere in the error of doing themselves what they do not understand, or of letting themselves be governed by incompetents. From that is often born the ultimate ruin of a city.

* * *

138. NEITHER FOOLS nor wise men can ultimately resist what must be. Hence, I have never read anything that I thought better said than: *Ducunt volentes fata, nolentes trahunt.*[25]

* * *

139. IT IS true that cities, like men, are mortal. But there is a difference. Men, being made of corruptible matter, will perish, even though they do nothing irregular. Cities do not perish from a defect in their substance, for that renews itself constantly. Rather they perish either because of bad fortune or because of bad government—that is to say, because of the imprudent measures taken by their rulers. Ruin through bad fortune alone is very rare. Being a vigorous body of such great resistance, it would take extraordinary and intense violence to destroy a city. The ruin of cities, then, is almost always caused by the mistakes of rulers. If a city were always well governed, it is possible that it would last forever, or at least have an incomparably longer life than has been the case hitherto.

* * *

140. TO SPEAK of the people is really to speak of a mad animal gorged with a thousand and one errors and confusions, devoid of taste, of pleasure, of stability.

* * *

141. YOU NEED not be surprised at our ignorance of things that happened in past ages, or of things that happen in the provinces and in far off places. If you think about it carefully, you

_____

[25] "Fate leads the willing, drags the unwilling."

will find we do not have any true information about the present
or about the things that happen every day in our own city.
Often there is such a dense cloud or a thick wall between the
palace and the market place that the human eye is unable
to penetrate it. When that is the case, the people will know as
much about what the rulers are doing or the reason for doing
it as they know about what is happening in India. And thus
the world is easily filled with erroneous and idle opinions.

*   *   *

142. ONE OF the greatest pieces of good fortune a man can
have is the chance to make something he has done in his own
interest appear to have been done for the common good. That
was what made the enterprises of His Catholic Majesty so
glorious. They were always undertaken for his own security
or power, but often they would appear to be done either to
strengthen the Christian faith or to defend the Church.

*   *   *

143. IT SEEMS to me that all historians without exception have
erred in leaving out of their writings many facts well known
to their contemporaries, simply because they presupposed everyone knew them. That is why we now lack information on so
many points in Roman, Greek, and all other history. For
instance, we lack information concerning the authority and
diversity among magistrates, the constitution of government,
the art of warfare, the size of cities, and many such things
well known in the time of the writers and therefore omitted
by them. They should have remembered that in time cities
perish and the memory of things is lost, and that the sole
purpose for writing history is to preserve the memories forever.
Then they would have taken more care to write so that someone born in a far distant age would have all those things as
much before his eyes as did those who were then present. That
is indeed the aim of history.

*   *   *

144. I WAS in Spain when the news came that the Venetians
had made an alliance with the king of France against His

Catholic Majesty.[26] Upon hearing it, Almazano, his Secretary, told me a Castilian proverb which says in effect that the thread breaks where it is weakest. What it means is that the weakest always get it in the neck; for men do not act according to reason or consideration for others. Rather each seeks his own advantage, and all agree to make the weakest suffer because he is the one they least fear. If you have to deal with those stronger than you, always remember this proverb, for it is a matter of everyday reality.

* * *

145. You can be sure that although human life is short, those who know how to take advantage of time and not waste it uselessly will have lots of time to spare. For the nature of man is very capacious, and those who are efficient and resolute will get many things done.

* * *

146. It is a great misfortune not to be able to have the good without first having to take the bad.

* * *

147. It is a mistake to think that the victory of a cause depends upon its justice, for we see the contrary every day. Not right, but prudence, strength, and good fortune bring victory. It is very true that right gives birth to a certain confidence, founded in the belief that God gives victory to the just cause; and that belief makes men ardent and obstinate, which qualities sometimes bring victory. Thus, having a just cause may be indirectly useful, but it is wrong to believe it can be of direct use.

* * *

148. Those who would finish a war too quickly often lengthen

[26] Emperor Maximilian supported the Holy League after the Battle of Ravenna. When it became clear to the Venetians that his territorial interests conflicted with theirs, they again began to look to the French. G. is referring to this Venetian movement toward the French in 1513.

it.[27] By not waiting for the necessary provisions or for the enterprise to mature properly, they make difficult what would have been easy. And for every day of time that they wanted to save, they often lose more than a month. What is even more, their haste may even cause great disaster.

* * *

149. THOSE WHO try to be tightfisted while waging war always end by spending more. For nothing requires a more boundless effusion of money than war. The greater the provisions, the quicker the undertaking will be ended. Failure to make such provisions, just to save money, will make the enterprise take longer and, what is more, will result in incomparably greater cost. Accordingly, nothing is more pernicious than waging a war by disbursing monies desultorily and without large amounts of cash at hand. For that is not the way to finish a war but to nourish it.

* * *

150. IF YOU have offended a man, do not trust or confide in him, even in a business deal which, if successful, would bring him profit and honor. There are some men for whom the memory of an offense can be so strong that it drives them to avenge themselves, even against their own self-interest—either because they value that satisfaction higher, or because passion so blinds them that they can no longer discern their own honor and profit. Keep this *ricordo* in mind, for many err on this score.

* * *

151. WHAT I said earlier about princes also applies to people with whom you must deal: always keep your eye not so much on what reason dictates they ought to do, as on what you can believe they will do, in view of their nature and their habits.

* * *

152. BE VERY careful before you plunge into any new enterprise,

27 In the margin, G. wrote: "Our fate at Cremona." He is referring to the haphazard and ill-executed attempt by the army of the League of Cognac to take Cremona, in 1526.

for once you are in you must go on. And once you are involved, you often have such great trouble that, had you foreseen even a fraction of it, you would have stayed a thousand miles away; but having embarked, you cannot turn back. This happens most frequently in the case of quarrels, factions, and wars. Before entering into these things, or indeed any others, no amount of reflection or care can be considered excessive.

*   *   *

153. IT SEEMS that ambassadors often take the side of the prince at whose court they are. That makes them suspected either of corruption or of seeking rewards, or at least of having been bedazzled by the endearments and kindnesses shown them. But the reason may also be that the ambassador has the affairs of that prince constantly before his eyes, and since he sees no others in as much detail, they assume greater importance than they really have. But the same is not true of the ambassador's own prince, whose distance allows him to see everything equally well. He quickly detects the mistakes of his minister and will often attribute to evil design what is more probably caused by bad judgment. If you are to become an ambassador, heed this well, for it is a matter of great importance.

*   *   *

154. INFINITE ARE the secrets of a prince; infinite the things to which he must attend. It is therefore rash to judge their actions hastily. Very often, what you think he has done for one reason, he has done for another; what you think done by chance or imprudently, is in fact done with great skill and profound wisdom.

*   *   *

155. IT IS said that anyone who does not know all the details well cannot judge well. And yet I have often seen it happen that someone of poor judgment will judge better if he knows only generalities than if he is shown the details. For on the general level, a proper conclusion will often present itself to him; but as soon as he hears all the details, he becomes confused.

*   *   *

156. I HAVE always been very resolute and firm in my actions. And yet, as soon as I make an important decision, I am often a little bit sorry for the stand I have taken. Not that I believe I would decide differently if I had it to do over again. The reason is, rather, that before the decision, I had present before my mind's eye the difficulties either choice would present; whereas having taken a stand and no longer fearing the difficulties inherent in the course I did not take, I become conscious only of those with which I must now deal. And those, considered by themselves, seem larger than they did when they were being compared with the others. To free yourself from this torment, you must diligently revive in your mind all those other difficulties you left behind.

* * *

157. To GET a reputation for being suspicious and distrustful is certainly not desirable. Nevertheless, men are so false, so insidious, so deceitful and cunning in their wiles, so avid in their own interest, and so oblivious to other's interests, that you cannot go wrong if you believe little and trust less.

* * *

158. You CAN see at every turn the benefits you derive from having a good name, a good reputation. But they are few compared to those you do not see. These come of their own accord, without your knowing the cause, brought about by that good opinion people have of you. It was said most wisely: a good name is worth more than great riches.

* * *

159. I DO NOT criticize fasting, prayers, and other pious works that are ordained by the Church or recommended by the monks. But the greatest good, compared to which all others are trifling, is to harm no one and to help everyone as much as you can.

* * *

160. IT IS certainly marvelous that although we all know we must die, we live as though we were sure to live forever. I do not believe this comes about because we are moved more by

what is before our eyes and appears to the senses than we are by things far off and invisable. For death is close, and we know from daily experience that it appears to us at every hour. I think the reason is that nature wants us to live according to the course, or the order, of this machine that is the world. Since nature did not want the world to remain inert and senseless, she gave us the property of not thinking about death, for if we did, the world would be full of sloth and torpor.

* * *

161. WHEN I consider the infinite ways in which human life is subject to accident, sickness, chance, and violence, and when I consider how many things must combine during the year to produce a good harvest, nothing surprises me more than to see an old man, a good year.

* * *

162. IN WARS as well as in many other important matters, I have often seen preparations neglected because they were thought to be too late. But later on, it became clear that they would have been in time and that dropping them caused great harm. This happens because generally things move much slower than planned; very often, you cannot get done in three or four months what you thought should be done in one. This is an important *ricordo* and one which you must heed.

* * *

163. How APT was that saying of the ancients: *Magistratus virum ostendit.*[28] Nothing reveals the quality of of a man more than to give him authority and responsibility. So many speak well but do not know how to do; so many on the benches or in the market place seem excellent men, but when employed, show themselves to be mere shadows.

* * *

164. A MAN's good fortune is often his worst enemy, for it can make him wicked, lighthearted, insolent. A man's ability to bear

[28] "The office reveals the man."

good fortune, therefore, is a far better test of him than his ability to bear adversity.

* * *

165. On the one hand, it would seem that a prince or a master should know the character of his subjects and servants better than anyone else because he has to deal with their wants, their ambitions, and their conduct. But in fact, the opposite is true. For they will deal quite openly with others, but with their master they will use the utmost care and every art to mask their character and their thoughts.

* * *

166. You must not suppose that whoever assumes the offensive —besieges a city, for instance—can foresee all of the defenses his enemy will devise. Naturally, the skillful aggressor will foresee the ordinary remedies to which the defender will resort. But danger and necessity will enable the defender to find extraordinary remedies, impossible to conceive, unless one were himself in the same straits.

* * *

167. I believe there is nothing worse in this world than levity. For lighthearted men are the ready instruments of any party, no matter how bad, dangerous, or pernicious. Therefore, flee from them as you would from fire.

* * *

168. What difference does it make if a man offends me out of ignorance rather than ill will? Indeed, it is often much worse, for ill will at least has its definite aims, functions according to its own rules, and therefore does not always hurt as much as it might. But ignorance, having neither aims nor rules nor standards, moves furiously and deals the blows of blind men.

* * *

169. Take it as a rule that whether you live in a republic, under an oligarchy, or under a prince, it is impossible to achieve every-

thing you plan. Therefore, if one of your plans falls through, do not fly into a rage or begin to plan rebellion—not, at least, so long as you still have a stake in the *status quo*. For if you do, you will upset yourself and perhaps even the whole city. And in the end, you will almost always find that you have worsened your position.

* * *

170. HAPPY IS the fate of princes. They can so easily unload on others the burdens that should be theirs. The errors and offenses they commit, and for which they are responsible, are nearly always attributed to bad advice or to the instigation of those around them. I think this is due not so much to the effort princes make to create that impression as it is to the fact that men prefer to hate and slander those less distant from them, against whom they can more easily hope to retaliate.

* * *

171. DUKE LUDOVICO SFORZA used to say that princes and crossbows could be tried by the same rule. Whether the crossbow is good is judged by the arrows it shoots. So too, the value of princes is judged by the quality of the men they send forth. We can guess, therefore, what sort of government there was in Florence when it employed as ambassadors simultaneously Carducci in France, Gualterotti in Venice, Bardi in Siena, and Galeotto Giugni in Ferrara.

* * *

172. PRINCES WERE ordained not for their own sake but for the common good, and their revenues and profits were meant to be used for the well-being of their dominions and their subjects. Parsimony, therefore, is more detestable in princes than in private citizens. For a prince who hoards wealth is appropriating to himself that over which, properly speaking, he was made, not master, but guardian and administrator for the benefit of many.

* * *

173. PRODIGALITY IN a prince is more detestable and more pernicious than parsimony. For a prince cannot be prodigal without

taking something from many of his subjects, and thus they are worse off than if he were parsimsious and gave them nothing. And yet it seems the public prefers a prodigal prince to a stingy one. The reason is that although the prodigality of the prince favors few men compared to the necessarily large number from which it takes, it is nevertheless true, as I have said at other times, that men hope more than they fear. They like to think they will be one of the few who will be favored rather than one of the many from whom something will be taken.

* * *

174. DO WHATEVER you can to be in good favor with princes and with those who rule. For even if you are innocent and are of a peaceful and orderly temperament, not disposed to agitation of any kind, things will inevitably happen that put you right into the hands of those who govern. And then the mere belief that you are not acceptable will hurt you in infinite ways.

* * *

175. A RULER, or someone endowed with executive power, must be very careful not to show hatred or take vengeance against anyone who offends him personally. For the use of the public arm against private offenses will subject him to heavy censure. Let him be patient and mark time. Inevitably he will have an opportunity to achieve the same effect justly and without a note of rancor.

* * *

176. PRAY TO GOD that you are always on the winning side, for you will get credit even for things in which you had no part. If, on the contrary, you are a loser, you will be blamed for an infinite number of things of which you are entirely innocent.

* * *

177. BECAUSE MEN are so foolish in Florence, it happens all too frequently that no attempt is made to punish those who have caused upheavals. Instead, every effort is made to grant them impunity, so long as they put down their arms and desist. This

sort of thing hardly serves to repress the insolent; on the contrary, it turns lambs into lions.

* * *

178. INDUSTRIES AND trades are at their best before many people recognize how profitable they are. As soon as that happens, they decline, for strong competition makes them less profitable. Thus, in all matters, it is wise to get up very early.

* * *

179. WHEN I was young, I used to scoff at knowing how to play, dance, and sing, and at other such frivolities. I even made light of good penmanship, knowing how to ride, to dress well, and all those things that seem more decorative than substantial in a man. But later, I wished I had not done so. For although it is not wise to spend too much time cultivating the young toward the perfection of these arts, I have nevertheless seen from experience that these ornaments and accomplishments lend dignity and reputation even to men of good rank. It may even be said that whoever lacks them lacks something important. Moreover, skill in this sort of entertainment opens the way to the favor of princes, and sometimes becomes the beginning or the reason for great profit and high honors. For the world and princes are no longer made as they should be, but as they are.

* * *

180. THE WORST enemy of someone who begins a war is his belief in easy victory. For no matter how simple and certain it appears, a war is subject to a thousand accidents. And the confusion these accidents create will be even greater if they happen to someone who has not prepared his mind and his forces for them—preparations he would have made if he had considered the war difficult from the start.

* * *

181. I WORKED in the government of the Papal State for eleven successive years and found such favor among both my superiors and the people that I would have stayed on for a long time,

had it not been for the events that occurred in Rome and Florence in 1527.[29] During that period, nothing rendered my position more secure than acting as though staying on were a matter of little concern to me. On that basis, without fear or submissiveness, I could carry out my duties properly. That in turn greatly enhanced my reputation. And from my reputation alone I derived far greater, more dignified service than I could ever have secured through any endearments, friendships, or other expedients.

* * *

182. I HAVE observed that when wise men must make an important decision, they nearly always proceed by distinguishing and considering the two or three most probable courses events will take. And on those they base their decision, as if one of the courses were inevitable. Take heed: this is a dangerous way to do things. Often—perhaps even the majority of times—events will take a third or fourth course that has not been foreseen and to which your decision is not tailored. Therefore, make your decisions as much on the safe side as possible, remembering that things can easily happen that should not have happened. Unless forced by necessity, do not restrict yourself.

* * *

183. IT IS very unwise for a captain to go into battle unless he is moved by necessity or by the knowledge that he has a great advantage. A battle is very subject to Fortune; and defeat is too important a matter ever to risk.

* * *

184. I DO NOT wish to deter men from talking together and discussing things with pleasant, loving familiarity. Nevertheless, I must say it is prudent not to talk about your own affairs except when necessary. And when you do speak of them, say no more than is necessary for your argument or your purpose, always

[29] In May 1527, Rome was sacked by an Imperial army. Clement VII shut himself up in Castel Sant' Angelo for a while but finally capitulated. In the same month, the Medici were expelled from Florence.

keeping to yourself everything you can. To do otherwise is more pleasant, but to do this is more useful.

* * *

185. MEN ALWAYS praise the lavish spending, the generosity, and magnificence of others. But in their own lives the majority of men practice just the opposite. Therefore, measure your expenditures by your means and by the profit they may honestly and reasonably bring. And do not be swayed by the opinions and words of the mob or by the belief that you will gain praise and reputation among them. When all is said and done, they will not praise in others what they do not practice themselves.

* * *

186. YOU CANNOT always abide by an absolute and fixed rule of conduct. Often it is unwise to be open in your conversations, even with your friends—I mean, on those matters that should be kept secret. On the other hand, to act with your friends in such a manner that they notice you are being reserved is to assure that they will do the same with you. For the only thing that makes others confide in you is the assumption that you confide in them. Thus, if you reveal nothing to others, you lose the possibility of knowing anything from them. In this, as in other matters, you must be able to distinguish the character of the person, of the case, and of the occasion; and for that, discretion is necessary. If discretion is not given by nature, it can rarely be learned adequately from experience. It can never be learned from books.

* * *

187. REMEMBER THIS: whoever lives a life of chance will in the end find himself a victim of chance. The right way is to think, to examine, and to consider every detail carefully, even the most minute. Even if you do, it takes great pains to make things come out right. Imagine how things must go for those who drift.

* * *

188. THE FURTHER you move from the center to avoid an ex-

treme, the more easily will you fall into the extreme you fear, or into an equally bad one. Likewise, the more you want to exploit what you own, the more quickly will you cease owning and exploiting it. Take the example of a people that enjoys liberty: the more they want to use it, the less will they enjoy it, and the sooner will they fall under a tyranny, or a state that is not much better than tyranny.

*   *   *

189. ALL CITIES, all states, all reigns are mortal. Everything, either by nature or by accident, ends at some time. And so a citizen who is living in the final stage of his country's existence should not feel as sorry for his country as he should for himself. What happened to his country was inevitable; but to be born at a time when such a disaster had to happen was his misfortune.

*   *   *

190. TO COMFORT those who are not what they would like to be, the proverb says: Look behind you and not before you. In other words, look how many more people there are worse off than you. It is a very true saying and should have the effect of making men happy with their lot. And yet it is very hard to accept, because nature placed our face in such a way that, unless we strain ourselves, we can only look ahead.

*   *   *

191. ONE SHOULD not criticize men who take long in making decisions. To be sure, things do sometimes happen that require quick decisions; but nevertheless, generally speaking, the man who decides quickly makes more mistakes than the man who takes his time. What is highly reprehensible is to be slow in executing a decision after it has been made. One might even say that such tardiness is always harmful and can never be useful except accidentally. I tell you this so that you may be on your guard, for this is a matter on which many err, either through laziness, or to avoid trouble, or for some other reason.

*   *   *

192. IN BUSINESS matters take this as a maxim: it is not enough

to begin things, give them their direction, and get them moving; you must also follow them up and stay with them until the end. If you do, you will have contributed much to their successful conclusion. Anyone who does business otherwise often assumes that a deal is concluded when in fact it is hardly begun, or has many obstacles before it. You should remember that the negligence, the ineptitude, and the wickedness of men are great, and that many impediments and difficulties are inherent in the very nature of things. Make use of this *ricordo*. It has, on occasion, brought me great honor, just as it brings disgrace to those who practice the contrary.

* * *

193. IF YOU are planning something against the state, be sure never to communicate it by letter, for often these letters are intercepted and they make incontestable testimony. And although there are now many secret ways of writing letters, there are also many arts for deciphering them. It is much safer to use your own men than letters. And for just that reason, it is too difficult and too dangerous for private citizens to get involved in such dealings, for they do not have many men whom they can so employ. And even those few they cannot trust, since there is much to be gained and little to be lost in betraying private citizens to please princes.

* * *

194. YOU SHOULD, of course, proceed cautiously in all matters. But you must not conjure up so many difficulties that you come to consider a job impossible and stop working at it. Indeed, you must remember that it is only by working at things that they become easy: and in the process of working, difficulties disappear of their own accord. This is very true, and men who have business to transact will witness it, in fact, every day. And if Pope Clement would remember it, he might often conduct his affairs more rapidly and more honorably.

* * *

195. IF SOMEONE at the court of a prince wants favors or advancement for himself or his friends, he must be very careful

not to ask for them directly very often. Rather he should seek or await occasions for proposing and introducing them adroitly. When these occasions come, he must take advantage of them immediately and not let them slip. If a man does this, he will get what he wants with very great ease and with little annoyance to the prince. Furthermore, having obtained one favor, he will be freer and better able to obtain another.

* * *

196. WHEN MEN see that your condition forces you to do their will, they have little respect and take advantage of you. For generally men's actions are more determined by their self-interest or by their evil character rather than by considerations of reason, of your merits, or of their obligations to you. Not even the thought that they caused you to fall upon evil days will temper their actions. Therefore, guard yourself against being in this humiliating condition as you would guard yourself against fire. If men had this *ricordo* well placed in their hearts and minds, many who are now exiled would still be here. It does a man no good to know that he was forced to leave his home because of loyalty to this or that prince; but it does him great harm to be far away and to have the prince in a position to say to himself: that man is powerless without me. For then the prince will pay no attention to him, and will treat him just as he pleases.

* * *

197. IF YOU have to deal with the public on matters that are very difficult, or contain contradictions, be careful to separate the issues, if at all possible, and not to speak of the second until the first is settled. If you do, it may happen that those who oppose the one will not oppose the other; whereas, if they were all together, the whole would be contradicted by anyone who was displeased with any part of it. If Piero Soderini had done this when he wanted to re-establish the law of the Quarantia, he would have obtained it, and perhaps been able to consolidate popular government with it.[30] This *ricordo* is just as useful in

[30] In Venice, the Quarantia was a special court made up of forty distinguished men to adjudicate important civil and criminal cases. The

private as in public affairs, if you want to get men to swallow
bitter pills in several gulps.

* * *

198. BELIEVE ME: in all matters, public or private, success depends on the right approach. Whether you succeed or fail in
an enterprise depends on whether you handle it one way or
the other.

* * *

199. IF YOU want to disguise or conceal one of your intentions,
always take pains to show you have its opposite in mind, using
the strongest and most convincing reasons you can find. If men
think you know what is reasonable, they will easily believe that
your decisions are going to follow the dictates of reason.

* * *

200. ONE OF the ways to make a supporter out of someone who
would otherwise be hostile to a plan of yours, is to make him
head of it and to make him think he were, so to say, its author
or director. Lighthearted men are generally won over by this
device because it flatters their vanity, and that is more important to them than real gains.

* * *

201. IT MAY seem a wicked or suspicious thing to say, and would
to God it were not true, but the fact is, there are more bad
men than good, especially in matters regarding property or
power. Therefore, except for those whom you know to be good
from experience or from a completely trustworthy source, it is
wise to deal with all people with your eyes wide open. If you
can do it without getting a reputation for being suspicious, so
much the better. But the important point is: don't trust anyone
unless you are sure you can.

* * *

---

judges were chosen by the Grand Council; but the Quarantia remained an
independent, stable, and highly respected organ of the state. Florence had
convened a Quarantine on occasion, but very rarely. By Soderini's time, it
was only a memory. It was, indeed, re-established in the republic after
1527, and it was the Court that condemned G. to exile *in absentia*.

202. IF YOU avenge yourself in such a manner that the injured party does not know whence the injury comes, you cannot be said to have done it for any reason but hatred or rancor. It is more honest to do it openly and in such a manner that everyone knows who did the deed. For then you can be said to have acted not so much out of hatred or the desire for revenge, as for the sake of honor. That is to say, you have done it so that others will know you are the sort of man who does not take insults.

* * *

203. PRINCES SHOULD beware of allowing their subjects too many liberties. For men naturally desire freedom; and human nature is such that men will never be satisfied with their condition but will always seek to improve it. These appetites are stronger than the memory of the good life or of the benefits received under the prince.

* * *

204. NO MATTER what you do, government employees will steal. I have been very honest; and yet, despite all my efforts and my good example, I could never quite stop the administrators and other officials who worked under me. The reasons are that money is useful in all things and that today a rich man is more respected than a good man. Another reason is the ignorance or ingratitude of princes, who tolerate evildoers and are not more generous to those who have served well than to those who have not.

* * *

205. TWICE I have had high posts in armies undertaking very important campaigns. And as a result, I have learned this lesson: if the things written about ancient armies are true—as for the most part I believe they are—then ours are a mere shadow by comparison. Modern captains have no vigor, no skill. They move without art, without strategy, as though they were walking slowly down a main street. When Prospero Colonna, captain of the first campaign, reminded me that I had never served in

a war before, I answered very pointedly that I was sorry to say I had learned nothing from this one.

* * *

206. I do not wish to discuss whether it is better to have physicians treat our bodies or to dispense with their services altogether, as the Romans did for a long time. It may be that the subject itself is difficult; or it may be that physicians, instead of observing keenly and carefully their patient's slightest symptom, are negligent: the fact remains that the physicians of our time do not know how to treat anything but common ailments. The best their science can do is cure a double tertian. But as soon as a sickness has something extraordinary about it, they are in the dark and treat you at random. Moreover, because of their ambition and because of the competition among them, physicians are awful creatures, without conscience and without scruples. They know their mistakes are hard to prove; and so, either to exalt themselves or to discredit their colleagues, they use our bodies daily for their anatomical experiments.

* * *

207. It is mad to believe in astrology—that is to say, in the sciences that judges future events. The science is either completely false, or else the things necessary for its practice are unknowable or unattainable by the human mind. But the result is the same: to think one can know the future by that means is a dream. Astrologers do not know what they are talking about; they are never right except by accident. If you take a prediction made by an astrologer and one made at random by another man, the latter has as much chance of turning out to be true as the former.

* * *

208. The science of law has come to such a pass that if one side of a case presents a cogent argument and the other presents the authority of a scholar who has written on the subject, more attention will be paid to the authority. And so practicing lawyers are forced to read everyone who has written, with the result that the time which should be devoted to reasoning is

consumed in reading books. And such reading is so fatiguing
to the mind and body that it is more like the work of a porter
than that of an educated man.

*   *   *

209. I THINK the Turkish practice of making legal decisions
expeditiously, and almost haphazardly, is not as bad as the way
Christians arrive at a judgment. For the latter involves so much
time, so much expense, and so much trouble to the litigants
that even the eventual winner of the case might find it more
profitable to have lost it on the first day. Moreover, even if we
suppose the sentences of the Turks to be passed entirely at
random, it follows that about half of them will be just. But
given the ignorance and the malice of our judges, it may well be
that fewer of the Turkish sentences are any more unjust than
ours.

*   *   *

210. "LITTLE AND GOOD," says the proverb. It is impossible for
someone who says or writes many things not to put in a good
deal of nonsense; whereas, few things can be well digested and
concise. And so it may have been better to select the best of
these *ricordi* rather than to have accumulated so much material.

*   *   *

211. I THINK I can affirm the existence of spirits—I mean those
things we call spirits, those airy ones who converse familiarly
with people. I have had the sort of experience with them that
makes me think I can be quite sure. But I believe that their
nature, what they are, is just as obscure to those who profess
to know as to those who never give it a thought. This knowledge
of spirits and the prediction of the future, which we sometimes
see people make either through their art or in a frenzy, are
occult potencies of nature—or rather, of that higher agent who
sets everything in motion. They are known to him, secret from
us; the minds of men cannot reach them.

*   *   *

212. OF THE three kinds of government—by the one, by the

few, or by the many—I believe that for Florence oligarchy would
be the worst. It is not natural to Florence and would be as
unacceptable as a tyranny. Indeed, ambition and discord among
the oligarchs would produce all the same evils as tyranny, and
perhaps more. They would quickly divide the city but do
none of the good things that a tyrant does.

* * *

213. IN ALL human decisions and actions there is always a reason
for doing the opposite of what we do, for nothing is so perfect
that it does not contain a defect. Nothing is so evil that it
does not contain some good, just as nothing is so good that it
does not contain some evil. This causes many men to remain
inactive, because every tiny flaw disturbs them. They are the
overconscientious, awed by every minute detail. That is no way
to be. Rather, having weighed the disadvantages of each side,
we should decide for the one that weighs less, remembering
that no choice is clear and perfect in every respect.

* * *

214. EVERYONE HAS faults, some more, some fewer. Neither
friendship nor service nor companionship can endure if one
man does not tolerate the other. We must learn to know one
another; we must remember that change will not eliminate all
defects, but that we will encounter the same or even greater
ones in a new situation. And so we must be tolerant—provided
that the issues concerned are such that they can be tolerated
or are not of great importance.

* * *

215. MANY ACTS are censured when they are done—and yet if
we could see what would have happened without them, they
would have been praised. And conversely, many acts are praised
which would otherwise have been censured. Do not let superficial realities and appearances lead you into hastily assigning
blame or lavishing praise. If you want your judgment to be
balanced and true, you must look deeply below the surface of
things.

* * *

216. IN THIS world, no one chooses the rank into which he will be born nor the circumstances and the fate with which he will have to live. And so, before praising or censuring men, you must not look at their condition but at how they manage within it. Praise or blame must be based on their behavior, not on the state in which they find themselves. In a comedy or a tragedy we do not have higher respect for the actor who plays the part of the master or the king than for the one who plays the servant. Instead, we pay attention only to the quality of the performance.

* * *

217. DO NOT be so wary of making enemies or of displeasing others that you neglect your obligations. Doing your duty brings you reputation, and that is more useful than making an occasional enemy is harmful. In this world, unless you are dead, you cannot avoid doing things occasionally that will offend someone. The same rule that guides us in giving pleasure to others also tells us when it is necessary to displease them: these things must be done reasonably, on the proper occasion, with modesty, with cause, and with honorable means.

* * *

218. IN THIS world of ours, the men who do well are those who always have their own interests in mind and measure all their actions accordingly. But it is a great error not to know where true interest lies; that is, to think it always resides in some pecuniary advantage rather than in honor, in knowing how to keep a reputation, and in a good name.

* * *

219. IF A MAN has made a decision or affirmed an opinion and then decides for some reason to change his mind before the decision has been implemented, it is very honest of him to confess it freely. But if it is not within his power or competence to change the effects of his original decision, he will keep his reputation better by sticking to it. By changing his mind he can only lose, because what takes place must necessarily be the

opposite of what he said at the beginning or of what he said later. But if he had stood by his first opinion, he would appear trustworthy if it proved to be true, as it well might.

*　*　*

220. WHENEVER A COUNTRY falls into the hands of a tyrant, I think it is the duty of good citizens to try to cooperate with him and to use their influence to do good and avoid evil. Certainly it is in the interests of the city to have good men in positions of authority at all times. Ignorant and passionate Florentines have always thought otherwise, but they should recognize how disastrous the rule of the Medici would be if there were no one around them but foolish and evil men.

*　*　*

221. IF YOUR enemies, who are usually united against you, have started fighting among themselves, attacking one of them in the hope of beating him separately may well cause them to reunite. Therefore, you must consider very carefully the measure of hatred born between them, as well as all other conditions and circumstances. Then you can decide properly which course is better: to attack one of them, or to stand aside and let them fight it out among themselves.

Series B

Although leisure alone does not give birth to whims, it is indeed true that there can be no whims without leisure.

1. CITIZENS WHO seek honor and glory in their city are praiseworthy and useful, provided they seek it not by faction or usurpation but by striving to be considered wise and good, and by serving their country. Would to God our republic were full of such ambition! But citizens whose only goal is power are dangerous. For men who make power their idol cannot be restrained by any considerations of honor or justice, and they will step on anything and everything to attain their goal.

* * *

2. IF A MAN is not really a good citizen, he will not long be thought one. And so even if he only wishes to give the impression of being a good citizen, he must nevertheless force himself to be one. Otherwise, in the end he will not even appear to be one.

* * *

3. MEN ARE naturally inclined to the good. Unless they can reap pleasure or advantage from evil, they prefer the good. But since human nature is fragile, and the temptations to do evil are infinite, men are easily deviated from their natural inclination by self-interest. For this reason, wise legislators discovered the spur and the bridle, that is to say, rewards and punishments—not to do violence to human nature but to maintain its natural propensity. When rewards and punishments are not used in a republic, you will very rarely find good citizens. In Florence we see it proved every day.

4. IF YOU hear or read of someone who prefers evil to good, without advantage or profit to himself, call him a beast, not a man. For he lacks an appetite that is naturally common to all men.

* * *

5. GREAT DEFECTS and failings are inherent in popular government. Nevertheless, the wise and good citizens of our city prefer it as a lesser evil.

* * *

6. WE MAY say, then, that in Florence a wise man is also a good citizen. For if he were not a good citizen, he would not be wise.

* * *

7. THE SORT of generosity that pleases the public is very seldom found in truly wise men. A man who appears generous, therefore, is not as praiseworthy as a judicious man.

* * *

8. IN A REPUBLIC the people love a just citizen. To the wise they accord their reverence rather than their love.

* * *

9. OH GOD! How many more reasons there are to believe our republic will soon fail than to think it will last a long time.

* * *

10. A MAN who has good sense can make great use of one who has many talents—much more than if it were the other way around.

* * *

11. THE EQUALITY of men under a popular government is by no means threatened if one citizen enjoys greater reputation than another, provided it proceed from the love and reverence of all, and can be withheld by the people at their pleasure. Indeed, without such props, a republic can hardly be maintained.

It would be a good thing for our city if the fools in Florence understood this well.

* * *

12. HE WHO must command others should not be too fastidious or scrupulous in giving orders. I do not say he should be without these qualities altogether, but too much is harmful.

* * *

13. YOU HAVE everything to gain from managing your affairs secretly. And you will gain even more if you can do it without appearing secretive to your friends. For many men feel slighted and become indignant when they see that you refuse to confide in them.

* * *

14. I WANT to see three things before I die, but I doubt whether I shall see any of them, no matter how long I live. I want to see a well-ordered republic in our city, Italy liberated from all the barbarians, and the world delivered from the tyranny of these wicked priests.

* * *

15. UNLESS YOUR safety is completely guaranteed by treaty or by such great strength that no matter what happens, you have nothing to fear, you are mad to stay neutral when others are at war. For you do not satisfy the vanquished, and you remain prey to the victor. If you are not convinced by reason, look at the example of our city and what happened to it by remaining neutral in the war that Pope Julius and the Catholic King waged against Louis, king of France.[1]

* * *

[1] The Holy League (Julius II, Ferdinand of Spain, and Venice) tried to drive the French from Italy. The young General Gaston de Foix led the French to a great victory at the Battle of Ravenna (April 11, 1512), where he lost his life. But the victory yielded few results for the French. Soon, they found themselves retreating toward the Alps. Florence had repulsed overtures from the League but given no help to the French. The Spaniards now demanded that Florence depose Piero Soderini and re-admit the Medici. When Florence refused, a Spanish army under Ramón de Cardona attacked Prato, a few miles north of Florence, and sacked the town thoroughly and brutally. Soderini resigned, and the Medici returned.

16. IF INDEED you want to remain neutral, at least make a pact of neutrality with the side that wants it, for that is one way of taking sides. And if they should win, they will perhaps be somewhat reluctant or ashamed to hurt you.

* * *

17. THERE IS far greater pleasure in controlling lewd desires than in gratifying them. The latter is brief and of the body; the former—once our appetite has somewhat subsided—is long lasting and of the mind and conscience.

* * *

18. HONOR AND reputation are more to be desired than riches. But since a reputation nowadays can scarcely be gained or maintained without riches, virtuous men should seek them—not immoderately, but just enough to acquire or preserve reputation and authority.

* * *

19. THE PEOPLE of Florence are generally poor. But our style of living is such that everyone wants very much to be rich. And so it is hard to preserve freedom in our city, for this appetite makes men pursue their personal advantage without respect or consideration for the public honor and glory.

* * *

20. THE MORTAR that holds together the rule of tyrants is the blood of citizens. Let everyone strive not to have such edifices constructed in his city.

* * *

21. IF THE CITIZENS of a republic are ruled by a government which—despite some defects—is tolerable, they should never try to change it for a better one. Nearly always the change will be for the worse. For he who makes the change will not have the power to fashion the new government precisely according to his designs and thoughts.

* * *

22. THE MAJORITY of crimes committed by the powerful men in cities arises from suspicion. Therefore, once a man has achieved power, the city is by no means obliged to those who try to tear him down without good reason. For that breeds suspicion, and that in turn brings the evils of tyranny.

* * *

23. AMONG THE POOR, malevolence may easily be caused by accident; in the rich it is more often there by nature. And so ordinarily it is more reprehensible in the rich than in the poor.

* * *

24. ANY ONE, WHETHER prince or private citizen, who wants to use an ambassador or some other representative to have others believe a lie, must first deceive the ambassador. For if he thinks he is representing the thoughts of his prince, an ambassador will act and speak more effectively than he would if he knew he were lying.

* * *

25. THE SUCCESS of very important matters often depends on doing or not doing something that seems trivial. Even in little things, therefore, you must be cautious and thoughtful.

* * *

26. IT IS very easy to ruin a good position, but very hard to acquire it. Therefore, if you are enjoying a good livelihood, make every effort not to let it slip through your fingers.

* * *

27. IT IS foolish to get angry with people whose power is so great that you can never hope to avenge yourself. Even if they offend you, therefore, grin and bear it.

* * *

28. IN A WAR an endless number of changes takes place from one minute to the next. Therefore, we must not be too encouraged by good news nor too depressed by bad, for often some

change will take place. And let those to whom opportunities present themselves during a war be herewith reminded not to lose them, for they last only a short time.

* * *

29. Just as it is often the fate of merchants to go bankrupt and of sailors to drown, so too those who govern territories of the church for any length of time generally come to a bad end.

* * *

30. The marquis of Pescara once said to me that things universally desired rarely happen. If this is true, the reason is that generally it is the few who set things in motion. And the objectives of the few are almost always contrary to the objectives and appetites of the many.

* * *

31. Never argue against religion or against things that seem to depend on God. These matters are too strongly rooted in the minds of fools.

* * *

32. It was said truly that too much religion spoils the world, because it makes the mind effeminate, involves men in thousands of errors, and diverts them from many generous and virile enterprises. I do not hereby wish to derogate from the Christian faith and divine worship, but rather to confirm and augment them by distinguishing what is excessive from what is sufficient, and by stimulating men's minds to consider carefully what should be taken into account and what may safely be ignored.

* * *

33. Any safeguard you can get against an enemy is good—his word, his promises, the word of his friends, or any other assurance. Still, given the low character of men and the fact that times change, nothing is better or surer than fixing things in such a way that you are safe, not because your enemy is unwilling, but because he is unable to hurt you.

* * *

34. YOU CAN have no greater good fortune in this world than to see your enemy prostrate on the ground before you, at your mercy. You should stop at nothing to attain that result, for it is indeed a great thing. But even greater is the glory of using such good fortune laudably, that is, by showing mercy and by forgiving. For these are qualities proper to generous and excellent men.

* * *

35. THESE *ricordi* are rules that can be written in books. But particular cases have different circumstances and must be treated differently. Such cases can hardly be written anywhere but in the book of discretion.

* * *

36. THE ANCIENTS had high praise for the proverb *Magistratus virum ostendit*. Not only do the responsibilities of office reveal whether a man be big or small, but even more, the power and freedom afforded by high position reveal the true bent of his spirit, the true nature of the man. For the more powerful a man is, the less will he hesitate or fear to be guided by what is natural to him.

* * *

37. BE CAREFUL not to fall into bad favor with the ruler of your country. Nor should you think that the manner and tenor of your life will prevent you from ever falling into his hands. For many unforeseen things can happen that will force you to need him.

Conversely, if a ruler wants to punish someone or avenge himself, he should not do it precipitously but ought to wait for the right time and occasion. For without doubt, in the long run an opportunity will come for him to satisfy his desire fully or partly without seeming wicked or passionate.

* * *

38. IF THE ruler of a city or of a people wants to keep them under control, he must be strict about punishing all crimes. But he may use mercy in the quality of the punishment. For,

aside from atrocious cases or those in which an example must be set, it is ordinarily quite sufficient to punish crimes at fifteen soldi to the lira.[2]

*   *   *

39. IF SERVANTS were respectful or grateful, it would be fitting and just for a master to benefit them as much as possible. But since they are usually just the opposite, and since they will either leave you or annoy you when they get their fill, it is better to ge tightfisted with them. Feed their hopes, but give them only just enough to keep them from despair.

*   *   *

40. THE ABOVE *ricordo* must not be applied in such a way that you acquire a reputation for being stingy, thus causing men to shun you. You can easily avoid that by occasionally being extraordinarily generous to one of them. For hope is naturally so dominant in men that a single instance of such generosity is more useful and brings you more credit among the others than a hundred instances of insufficient remuneration brings you discredit.

*   *   *

41. MEN REMEMBER offenses longer than favors. Indeed, even if they remember the favor at all, they will consider it to be smaller than it really was and will believe they deserved more than they got. The opposite is true of offenses; they always hurt more than they reasonably should. Therefore, other things being equal, be careful not to please one man if you must thereby equally displease another. For the reason just stated, you will, on the whole, lose more than you gain.

*   *   *

42. YOU CAN better rely on someone who needs you or who happens to have a common objective than on someone you have benefited. For men are generally not grateful. If you do not want to be deceived, make your calculations according to this rule.

*   *   *

[2] The lira was worth twenty cents.

43. I HAVE written the preceding *ricordi* so that you may know how to live and how to weigh things, and not to stop you from benefiting others. Because, aside from being a generous thing and the act of a noble spirit, it also happens occasionally that a benefit will be repaid—sometimes even to such an extent that makes up for many others. It is quite possible that the Power above us likes noble actions and therefore will not consent to their always being fruitless.

* * *

44. STRIVE TO have friends, for they can be useful to you in times, places, and situations you would never have foreseen. This *ricordo* may seem trite, but its proper value can be truly appreciated only by those who have learned it from some important experience.

* * *

45. A TRUTHFUL, open nature is universally liked and is, indeed, a noble thing; but it can be harmful. Deception, on the other hand, is useful and sometimes even necessary, given the wickedness of man; but it is odious and ugly. Thus, I do not know which to choose. I suppose you ought ordinarily to embrace the one without, however, abandoning the other. That is to say, in the ordinary course of events practice the former so that you will gain a reputation for being a sincere person. And nevertheless, on certain important and rare occasions, use deception. If you do this, your deceptions will be more useful and more successful because, having a reputation for sincerity, you will be more easily believed.

* * *

46. FOR THE above reasons, I cannot praise those who always live by deception and wiles; but I can excuse those who use them occasionally.

* * *

47. YOU MAY be sure of this: if you want to hide something you have done or attempted, it is always a good idea to deny it,

even if it is about to be discovered and become public. A forceful denial may not convince those who have evidence or believe the contrary, but it will at least raise some doubts.

* * *

48. IT IS incredible how useful secrecy is to a ruler. Not only can his plans be blocked or upset if they are known, but what is more, ignorance of them keeps men awed and eager to observe his every move. His slightest act will cause a thousand comments, which in turn bring great reputation. A ruler should accustom himself and his ministers to be silent not only about things which should not be known but even about all those things which there is no advantage in making public.

* * *

49. THE *ricordo* that warns against revealing secrets unless forced by necessity applies to everyone. For you become a slave to those who know your secrets—aside from all of the other evils that knowledge of them can bring about. Even when necessity forces you to tell them, you should do so as late as possible. For when men have lots of time, they will think a thousand and one evil thoughts.

* * *

50. To GIVE vent occasionally to feelings of pleasure or anger is very comforting, but it is harmful. Therefore, it is wise not to do it, even though it is very hard.

* * *

51. WHEN I was ambassador to Spain, at the court of the wise and glorious King Ferdinand of Aragon, I observed that whenever he wanted to embark on some new enterprise, or indeed when he wanted to get anything done, he did not announce it publicly first and then justify it. He did just the opposite. He managed things so craftily that before long, everyone was proclaiming: "The king must do such and so, for these reasons" —even before anyone knew what he had in mind. Then he would announce his intention to do what everyone already

deemed just and necessary. And his decisions would be received with incredible favor and praise.

* * *

52. SOME MEN attribute everything to prudence and virtue and try to ignore fortune. But even they cannot deny that it is a great stroke of luck to be around at a time when your virtues and the things you do best are highly valued. We see from experience that the same virtues are rated higher at one time and lower at another; the same act will be pleasing at one time, displeasing at another.

* * *

53. I DO NOT wish to discourage those men whose burning love of country would let them run great risks to lead it back to freedom. But I must say that in our city anyone who tries to change the regime to further his own interests is not wise, for it is a very risky business and, quite clearly, few plots succeed. Furthermore, even if you do succeed, it almost always happens that you do not attain even nearly what you had envisaged. Besides, you will be in a state of perpetual worry, for you must always fear that those you have driven out will return and undo you.

* * *

54. DO NOT waste your time with a revolution whose only result is to substitute one face by another. Are you any better off if the wrongs that used to be committed against you by Peter are now committed by Martin? To take an example: what pleasure can it give you to see Messer Goro go, if someone else of the same sort takes his place? [3]

* * *

55. IF YOU insist on getting mixed up in plots, remember that nothing undoes them more surely than the wish to make them too safe. For that takes more time, involves more men, and

[3] Goro Gheri, servant of the Medici, became secretary of Lorenzo, Duke of Urbino, after the restoration of 1512. He played a prominent part in Florentine Politics until Lorenzo's death in May, 1519.

gets more complicated. And these things in turn cause such plots to be discovered. You should also consider that Fortune, who dominates such matters, gets annoyed with anyone who tries that hard to free himself from her power and to safeguard himself against her. I conclude, therefore, that it is safer to execute the plot with some risks than with too many precautions.

* * *

56. DON'T EVER make plans on the basis of things you don't have; and don't spend your future earnings, because they often fail to materialize. Most of the time, it is clear, great merchants go bankrupt precisely for this reason. In the hope of making great profits in the future, they will take out notes, the interest for which is certain and has a definite time. But often the profits fail to come or take longer than had been anticipated. And thus an enterprise you had thought profitable becomes ruinous.

* * *

57. DO NOT believe those who tell you they have left public life because they love peace and quiet and are tired of ambition. They nearly always have just the opposite sentiment in their hearts and have been reduced to retirement either because of anger, necessity, or folly. We see examples of it every day. As soon as you give such people the slightest chance to return to power, they abandon their much-vaunted peace and quiet, and seize it with the same fury that fire seizes dry or oily things.

* * *

58. IF YOU have run afoul of the law, give every detail careful thought before you go away to prison. Although the case may be hard to prove, you cannot believe the number of things that can be thought up by a diligent judge anxious to prove the case. And even the tiniest opening is enough to bring everything to light.

* * *

59. LIKE OTHER men, I have pursued honor and profit. And hitherto, thanks be to God and to my good fortune, I have attained them beyond my hopes. But I never found in any of those things the satisfaction I had imagined. A good reason, if it be well considered, for men to still much of their thirst.

*   *   *

60. EVERYONE WANTS to achieve a high position, because everything that is good about it appears on the surface, whereas all the evil lies hidden within. If men could but see the evil, they might not be so eager; for a high position is undoubtedly full of dangers, suspicions, and a thousand and one worries and troubles. Perhaps its appeal, even to pure souls, stems from the universal desire to be superior to other men—especially since in that way more than any other we can resemble God.

*   *   *

61. UNANTICIPATED EVENTS affect us incomparably more than those we foresee. For that reason, I call a spirit great and dauntless if it can hold up and not be overcome by sudden dangers and accidents. It is, in my opinion, a very rare thing indeed.

*   *   *

62. IF WE could know what would have happened had a deed not been done or if the contrary had been done, many things now censured or praised by men would be found to deserve the opposite judgment.

*   *   *

63. THERE IS no doubt that avarice increases with age. The cause is commonly said to be that with age the mind gets weaker. But that hardly seems convincing to me, for an old man would have to be very stupid not to recognize that his needs diminish as he grows older. Moreover, I have observed in old men, at least in many of them, the continual growth of lechery (the appetite, not the power), cruelty, and other vices.

I believe the explanation may be that the longer men live, the
more they become accustomed to the things of this world, and
consequently they get to love them more.

*   *   *

64. FOR THE same reason, the older a man gets, the more oppres-
sive becomes the thought of death. And so more and more he
thinks and acts as though he were sure to live forever.

*   *   *

65. IT IS generally believed, and it is often seen from experience, that a dishonestly acquired fortune does not pass beyond
the third generation. Saint Augustine says that God permits the
man who has acquired the wealth to enjoy it in return for whatever good he has done in his lifetime. But then it may not pass
on very far, for God has so ordained against ill-gotten property.
I once told my father that another reason occurred to me. Generally the man who acquires the fortune, having been reared
in poverty, loves it and knows the art of keeping it intact. But
his children and grandchildren, having been reared in wealth,
quickly dissipate it. For they have no idea what it means to
earn a fortune, nor do they know how to keep it.

*   *   *

66. NO ONE can censure the desire to have children, for it is
natural. But I must say that it is a kind of luck not to have
any, for even good and wise children are undoubtedly more
trouble than comfort. I saw that to be the case with my father,
who, in his day, used to be cited in Florence as the example
of a father blessed with good sons. Think how it must be for
those who have bad ones.

*   *   *

67. I DO NOT condemn entirely the civil justice of the Turks,
which is hasty rather than summary. For even a man who
judges with his eyes closed will probably decide half the cases
justly and free both sides from expense and waste of time. But
our judges carry on in such a way that often the winning side

would have been better off with an unfavorable judgment on the first day rather than a favorable one after so much cost and trouble. Moreover, our judges are so wicked and ignorant, and our laws are so obscure, that even among us white is all too often made to seem black.

* * *

68. IT IS a mistake to believe that cases left by law to the discretion of a judge are placed before his will and whim. The law did not give him power so that he might show favor. Rather certain cases are left to his discretion—that is to say, to his synteresis, to his conscience—because the law cannot cover every single case, given the differences in circumstances. And so the judge must consider all the facts and do what seems just. This latitude in the law absolves him from having to account to the courts, for since his decision is not determined by law, he can always excuse himself. But it does not empower him to give away other people's property.

* * *

69. WE SEE from experience that masters take little account of their servants, and will get rid of them or humiliate them whenever they like. Therefore, servants are wise to do the same to their masters—always maintaining, of course, their integrity and their honor.

* * *

70. YOUNG MEN should realize that experience teaches a great deal—and more to large minds than to small. Anyone who thinks about it will easily see the reason.

* * *

71. EVEN THOUGH nature has endowed you with an excellent mind, you cannot arrive at or understand certain things without the experience that alone teaches them. This *ricordo* will be better appreciated by men who have managed many affairs, because they will have learned the value of experience from experience itself.

* * *

72. WITHOUT DOUBT, a prodigal prince is more popular than a tightfisted one. And yet it should be the contrary, for the prodigal prince must resort to extortion and rapacity, whereas the other takes from no one. Many more are the men who suffer from the exactions of a prodigal prince than those who benefit from his generosity. In my judgment, the explanation lies in the fact that hope is stronger than fear, and thus there are more men who hope to obtain something from him than those who fear his oppression.

* * *

73. BEING ON good terms with your brothers and relatives brings you an infinite number of benefits that you do not recognize, because you do not see each one by itself. It is advantageous to you in innumerable ways, and it makes men hesitate to offend you. Therefore, you should preserve their esteem and their love, even at the cost of some occasional inconvenience. Men often go wrong in this matter. They will resent the petty inconveniences that can be seen and disregard the great advantages that are not seen.

* * *

74. IF YOU have authority and rank over others, you can transgress and push beyond the limits of your sphere of authority. For subordinates cannot see and cannot measure what you may or may not do. Indeed, very often they will believe your strength to be greater than it is and will submit to things you could not have forced them to do.

* * *

75. I WAS once of the opinion that I could see things just as clearly at the start, as I could after a great deal of thought. But with experience, I have recognized that to be very false. And you may scoff at whoever tells you otherwise. The more you think about things, the more you understand them and the better you do them.

* * *

76. WHEN YOU have a chance to get something you want, take it without hesitation. For things change so often in this world that you cannot be said to have something until you have it in

your hand. For the same reason, when something is proposed that displeases you, try to put it off as long as you can. For, as you can see at every hour of the day, time brings accidents that get you out of your troubles. That is the meaning of the proverb whih wise men are always quoting: one must take advantage of the benefits of time.

* * *

77. SOME MEN always have high hopes of getting what they want; others never believe it until it is completely certain. Without doubt, it is better to have too little than too much hope. For too much hope makes you lessen your efforts and makes you sadder when your hope is not realized.

* * *

78. IF YOU want to know the thoughts of tyrants, read Cornelius Tacitus, where he cites the last conversations of Augustus with Tiberius.

* * *

79. IF YOU read him well, you will see that the same Cornelius Tacitus also teaches very admirably how those who live under tyrants should conduct themselves.

* * *

80. HOW WISELY was it said *Ducunt volentes fata, nolentes trahunt*. There are so many daily proofs of it, that, so far as I am concerned, truer words were never spoken.

* * *

81. THE TYRANT will make every effort to discover your views and to know whether you are content with his government. He will observe your movements, he will pump those who talk with you, he will discuss various things with you, proposing questions and asking your opinion. If you want to hide your thoughts, you must guard yourself with great care against the means he uses. You must not use terms that might arouse suspicion; you must watch what you say even to your close friends;

and you must speak and reply to him in such a way that he cannot catch you. If you always keep in mind that he is doing everything possible to ensnare you, you will succeed.

*   *   *

82. IF YOU are a man of rank who lives under a bloody and bestial tyrant, there is little good advice anyone can give you except to go into exile. But if the tyrant behaves decently, either out of prudence or necessity, or because of the circumstances of his position, you should strive to be highly respected and to be thought courageous but of a quiet nature, not anxious to change things unless forced. In that case, the tyrant will treat you gently and try not to give you any cause to think of making innovations. But he would not do that if he thought you were restless. In that case, knowing you would not keep still no matter what he did, he would be forced to look for an occasion to extinguish you.

*   *   *

83. IN THE above case, it is better not to be among the tyrant's confidants. For not only will he treat you gently, but in many matters he will take fewer liberties with you than he would with his friends. Thus you can enjoy his power, and if he should be overthrown, you can become powerful yourself. This *ricordo* is of no use to anyone who does not enjoy an important position in his country.

*   *   *

84. THERE IS a difference between desperate subjects and discontented subjects. The former think of nothing but revolutions and will try them even at great risk to themselves. The latter, though they may desire changes, will await but not invite occasions.

*   *   *

85. THE WICKEDNESS of men is such that you cannot govern well without severity. But you must be clever about it. You must do everything possible to have people believe that you dislike

cruelty and that you use it only out of necessity and for the public welfare.

* * *

86. MEN SHOULD look at the substance of things and not at their appearance or their surface. Nevertheless, it is incredible what favor you will gain among men by using gentle words and bestowing compliments. The explanation, I think, is that every man thinks he is worth more than he really is. And therefore he will be annoyed if he thinks you are not taking the account of him that he believes he deserves.

* * *

87. IT IS an honorable and manly thing not to promise what you cannot deliver. But since men are generally not governed by reason, anyone you reject, no matter how justly, will be dissatisfied. The opposite is the case when you promise things freely. For often accidents will happen that make it unnecessary for you to keep your promise. In that case, you have given satisfaction with nothing. Besides, even if you have to deliver, there are always excuses; and many people are so silly that they can be fooled by words. Nevertheless, going back on your word is an ugly thing, more important than any advantage you may draw from it. You should try, therefore, to put people off with evasive and encouraging answers, avoiding as far as possible a definite promise.

* * *

88. YOU SHOULD guard yourself against doing anything that can bring you harm but no profit. And so you should never speak ill of any man, absent or present, unless it be advantageous or necessary. For it is madness to make enemies without reason. I remind you of this because nearly everyone is guilty of this sort of levity.

* * *

89. A MAN who faces danger without considering the consequences must be called bestial. But brave is he who recognizes the danger and faces it squarely by reason of necessity or honor.

90. MANY BELIEVE that a wise man cannot be brave, because he sees all the dangers; I believe the opposite: that a timid man cannot be wise. For if he estimates a danger to be greater than it is, he is lacking in judgment. To clear up this confused issue, let me point out that not all dangers materialize. Some of them can be avoided by effort, industry, or courage. Others will be swept away by chance and the thousand and one accidents that take place. Therefore, to recognize dangers is not to say they are certain. After carefully reviewing all possible sources of help and the places where chance will be likely to favor him, a man should take courage and not withdraw from manly and honorable enterprises for fear of all the dangers he knows he must run.

* * *

91. IT IS a mistake to say that learning spoils the minds of men. Perhaps it is true in the case of weak minds. But learning imposed on a good mind makes it perfect. For a good natural endowment joined with good learning forms a most noble combination.

* * *

92. PRINCES WERE not ordained for their own benefit, for no one would have submitted to servitude without a purpose. They were ordained in the interests of the people, so that they might be well governed. Thus, when a prince ceases to respect the people, he is no longer a prince but a tyrant.

* * *

93. AVARICE IN a prince is incomparably more detestable than in a private citizen. That is true not only because the greater resources of a prince can deprive men of correspondingly more, but also because what a private citizen owns is all his and for his own use. He may dispose of it as he wishes without legitimate complaint from anyone. But what a prince has is given to him for the use and benefit of others, and by keeping it for himself, he defrauds men of their due.

* * *

94. I SAY that the duke of Ferrara's interests in business are not

only shameful but make him a tyrant. For he is usurping what belongs to private citizens, not to him. And with that, he sins as much against the people as they would sin against him if they were to interfere in the affairs of a prince.

* * *

95. CONSIDERING its origin carefully, all political power is rooted in violence. There is no legitimate power, except that of republics within their own territories but not beyond. Not even the power of the emperor is an exception, for it is founded on the authority of the Romans, which was a greater usurpation than any other. Nor do I except the priests from this rule—indeed, their violence is double, for they use both the temporal and the spiritual arms to subjugate us.

* * *

96. THE THINGS of this world are so unstable, and depend upon so many accidents, that it is very hard to form any judgment concerning the future. We see from experience that the predictions of wise men are nearly always wrong. Therefore, I cannot go along with those who would leave the comfort of a present, minor good, for fear of a future, greater evil, unless the latter be very close and very certain. For the thing you feared often does not happen, and then you find you have given up a pleasant thing needlessly. It is a wise proverb that says *di cosa nasce cosa*: one thing leads to another.

* * *

97. IN DISCUSSIONS of state, I have often seen men make mistakes when they judged what this or that prince will do according to reason, and not what he will do according to his nature and his character. If you want to judge, for instance, what the king of France will do, you must pay more attention to the nature and customs of a Frenchman than to how a prudent man should act.

* * *

98. I HAVE said it many times, and I say it again: a talented man, one who knows how to make good use of time, should

not complain that life is short. For he can attend to an infinite number of things; and knowing how to use time efficiently, he will have time to spare.

* * *

99. IF YOU want to work, do not allow any deals to be taken away from you. For one deal leads to another, both because the first paves the way for the second and because of the reputation you get by being actively in business. And so, in this respect too, you may adopt the proverb "one thing leads to another."

* * *

100. IT IS hard enough to think up these *ricordi,* but it is even harder to put them into practice. For very often men will not act on their knowledge. And so, if you want to make use of them, work on yourself. Develop good habits, by means of which you will be able not only to use the *ricordi* but also to do what reason commands without difficulty.

* * *

101. NO ONE will be surprised at the servile spirit of our citizens when he reads in Cornelius Tacitus how the Romans, who ruled the world and lived in such glory, served so basely under the emperors that Tiberius, a tyrannical and proud man, was disgusted by their worthlessness.

* * *

102. IF YOU are displeased with someone, try as hard as you can not to make him notice it, for it will alienate him from you completely. And often situations arise in which he could and would serve you, had you not lost him by showing your displeasures. I have had experience of this to my own profit. On occasion, I have been ill disposed towards someone who did not perceive it and who later served me well in various situations, as a good friend.

* * *

103. THINGS DESTINED to die not by a single blow but by gradual decay last much longer than people believe at first. That is

so because things move much more slowly than one thinks; and also because, when men hold out stubbornly, they can tolerate and accomplish much more than anyone would have believed. We see, for example, that a war we think will end because of famine, lack of supplies, lack of money, and the like, always lasts much longer than we anticipated. In like manner, consumptives always live longer than doctors and those around them predict. And a merchant can hold out longer than people think, before he is driven to bankruptcy by interest on his notes.

*　　*　　*

104. THOSE WHO deal with the great must be careful not to have their heads turned up by the blandiloquence and blandishments such people generally employ to choke men with favor and make them jump when they want. The harder it is to resist, the more you must try to control yourself, to keep a cool head, and not to let yourself be easily swayed.

*　　*　　*

105. THERE CAN be no greater virtue than to hold honor dear. Men who do will fear no danger nor commit any unseemly act. Keep this firmly in mind, and it will be almost impossible for your affairs not to go well: *Expertus loquor.*

*　　*　　*

106. YOU MAY scoff at men who preach liberty. Not at all of them, to be sure, but nearly. If they thought they would be better off under a tyranny, they would rush into it posthaste. For self-interest prevails in almost all human beings, and those who recognize the value of honor and glory are few.

*　　*　　*

107. I HAVE always found it difficult to believe that God would permit the children of Duke Ludovico to enjoy the state of Milan—not so much because he usurped it so outrageously as because in doing so he brought about the servitude and ruin of all Italy and the many attendant troubles throughout Christendom.

*　　*　　*

108. I SAY that a good and loyal citizen should seek to maintain good relations with the tyrant not only for his own safety—since he would be in danger if he were under suspicion—but also for the benefit of his country. For if he does, he will be able, through word and deed, to help many good causes and to hinder many evil ones. Those who censure him are mad; they and their city would be in a fine situation if the tyrant had no one but wicked men around him.

* * *

109. WHEN FLORENCE is not in a position to subjugate Siena, it is in our interest that there be wise government in that city. A wise man will always deal with us gladly; he will be guided more by reason than by the natural hatred the Sienese harbor against us, and he will not be eager to bring war to Tuscany. But now that the papacy is ours, it would be better if Siena were unwisely governed, for thus it would more easily fall into our mouths.

* * *

110. EVERYONE KNOWS that if the pope takes Ferrara, the object of future popes will always be lordship over Tuscany. The kingdom of Naples, being in the hands of strong princes, is too difficult for them.

* * *

111. UNDER A POPULAR government, it is to the advantage of houses like ours that the great houses be preserved. We profit from their being odious to the people. If they were to be annihilated, the hatred of the people would turn to the likes of us.

* * *

112. MY FATHER gave excellent advice to Piero Soderini when he told him to restore the Medici among us as private citizens. That step would have rid us of the exiles, the worst thing a state can have. And at the same time it would have stripped the Medici of their power both within and without the city. Within,

because they themselves would not have lived here willingly if they returned and saw they had to be the same as everyone else. Without, because the princes who believed the Medici had many partisans in the city would now see them return and be powerless, and thus they would no longer respect them. But I do not know whether my father's advice could have come out right without a brighter and braver gonfalonier than Piero Soderini.[4]

* * *

113. THE NATURE of peoples, like that of individuals, is such that they always want more than they have. It is wise, therefore, to deny them their first demand. For you cannot stop them by giving in. In fact, your concessions will invite them to ask for more and with greater insistence than before. The more you give them to drink the thirstier they get.

* * *

114. PAST EVENTS shed light on the future. For the world has always been the same, and everything that is and will be, once was; and the same things recur, but with different names and colors. And for that reason, not everyone recognizes them—only those who are wise, and observe and consider them diligently.

* * *

115. IN THIS world it is undoubtedly true that men of mediocre mind have a better time, a longer life, and are in some respects

---

[4] G. is reflecting the general opinion of Soderini's mediocrity, well expressed in Machiavelli's epigram:

> La notte che morì Pier Soderini,
> L'alma n'andò dell' inferno alla bocca;
> E Pluto le gridò: Anima sciocca.
> Che inferno? Va nel limbo dei bambini.

> The night that Piero Soderini died,
> His soul went to the gates of hell.
> And Pluto cried: Silly soul,
> What are you doing in hell? Go
> To the limbo of children.

happier than men of high intellect; for a noble mind is apt to be the cause of trouble and worry. But mediocre men participate more in brute animality than in humanity, whereas the others transcend the human condition and approach the celestial natures.

*　*　*

116. THE ACUTE observer will find that, from one age to another, not only do words, fashions, and manners change, but—more important—so do the tastes and inclinations of men's minds. This sort of diversity is observable even within the same age among different countries. I am not only speaking of manners, for they may proceed from differences in institutions, but of the different tastes in foods and of the appetites among men.

*　*　*

117. AN ENTERPRISE that is difficult or impossible if undertaken at the wrong time will prove to be very easy if undertaken at the right time and occasion. If you undertake things at the wrong time, you will find not only that they do not succeed but also that you risk spoiling them even for the time at which they might easily have succeeded. That is why wise men are said to be patient.

*　*　*

118. IN MY various administration posts I have observed that whenever disputes came before me which for one reason or another I wanted to settle, I never mentioned a settlement. Instead, by proposing various postponements and delays, I caused the parties to seek a settlement themselves. And thus, a proposal which would have been refused had I made it at the start, came to appear so attractive at the proper time that they would beg me to make it.

*　*　*

119. IT IS hardly surprising that a ruler who frequently resorts to cruelty and severity is feared. For subjects will surely fear someone who can hurt or ruin them and who does not hesitate

to do so. But I praise those rulers who, with little severity and few punishments, know how to acquire and preserve a reputation for terror.

* * *

120. I DO NOT say that a ruler is not sometimes forced to bloody his hands, but I do say that it ought never to be done except when absolutely necessary. And I will add that most of the time it brings more loss than gain. For not only does he offend those whom he attacks, but he displeases many others besides. And though he may have rid himself of one enemy and one obstacle, he has not destroyed the seed. Others will arise in the place of that one; and it often happens, as with the heads of Hydra, that seven grow for each one destroyed.

* * *

121. REMEMBER WHAT I said before: these *ricordi* should not be followed indiscriminately. In some particular case that presents different circumstances, they are of no use. Such cases cannot be covered by any rule, nor is there any book that teaches them. Rather, such illumination must be given you first of all by nature and then by experience.

* * *

122. CERTAINLY, NO position or office requires more prudence and excellence than the command of an army. For there are an infinite number of things a captain must foresee and control. And infinite, too, are the various accidents and chances that present themselves from one hour to the next. He truly needs more eyes than Argus. Both for the importance of the job in itself and for the prudence it demands, I consider a captaincy to be a burden compared to which any other is light.

* * *

123. To SPEAK of the people is to speak of a madman, a monster full of confusion and errors, whose vain opinions are as far from the truth as Spain, according to Ptolemy, is from India.

* * *

124. NATURALLY, I have always wanted to see the ruin of the

Papal State. But as fortune would have it, I have been forced to support and work for the power of two popes. Were it not for that, I would love Martin Luther more than myself, in the hope that his sect might demolish, or at least clip the wings, of this wicked tyranny of the priests.

* * *

125. THERE IS a difference between a brave man and one who faces danger out of regard for honor. Both recognize danger; but the former believes he can defend himself against it, and if he did not, he would not face it. The latter may even fear the danger more than he should, but he stands firm—not because he is unafraid but because he has decided he would rather suffer harm than shame.

* * *

126. IT OFTEN happens in our city that enmity will arise between the man who has taken over the government and the man who was his principal supporter. The cause is said to be that he who controls the government becomes suspicious of such men, since they are generally persons of quality and talent, and perhaps even restless. Another cause may be added: since such supporters think they have earned a great deal, they often want more than their due and are offended if they do not get it. And from that arises enmity and suspicion.

* * *

127. WHEN A man who has aided or caused someone to come to power then wants to tell him how to govern, he begins to cancel the help he has given. For he wants to make use of the authority which he helped the other to acquire. The man in power has just cause for not tolerating this; nor does he deserve to be called an ingrate.

* * *

128. LET US not praise anyone for doing or not doing something which, had it been omitted or done, would deserve censure.

* * *

129. THE CASTILIAN proverb says: "The thread breaks where it is weakest." In any contest or comparison of who is more power-

ful or more to be feared, the weaker will succumb, even though reason, honesty, or gratitude might dictate the contrary. For generally men have higher respect for their interests than for their duty.

* * *

130. I DO NOT know how to make myself appear in a flattering light nor how to gain a reputation for things that are not true. And yet it would be better if I did. For it is incredible how useful it is to have men believe that you are powerful. On the basis of that reputation alone they will run after you, without your having to prove a thing.

* * *

131. I HAVE often said it is more surprising that the Florentines should have acquired the little territory they have than that the Venetians or other Italian princes should have acquired their great holdings. For liberty was so rooted in every corner of Tuscany that Florentine aggrandizement was opposed everywhere. That has not been the case with those states situated among peoples accustomed to servitude and to whom it matters little whether they are dominated by one power or another. Such peoples never offer obstinate or long-lasting resistance. Furthermore, the vicinity of the Church has been and is a very great obstacle to Florence; for the Church, having its roots as deeply planted as it does, has very much impeded the course of our dominion.

* * *

132. EVERYONE AGREES that government by one good man is better than government by the few or the many, even if they too be good men. The reasons are obvious. Everyone also agrees that government by one man can more easily turn bad than the others; and when it is bad, it is the worst form of all. This change is especially easy since such government passes by inheritance, and very rarely does a good and wise father have a similar son. I wish that these political thinkers, considering all of the conditions and dangers, would have explained to me

which is more desirable for a new city: to be subject to the rule of one, of the many, or of the few.

*   *   *

133. A MASTER knows less about his servants than does anyone else; and the same is true of a ruler and his subjects. For they do not show themselves to him the same way they do to others. With him, they try to disguise themselves, and in fact try to seem completely different from what they really are.

*   *   *

134. IF YOU live at court or are the follower of a great prince, and you wish to be employed by him in his affairs, you must try to be constantly before his eyes. For matters will arise suddenly, which he will commit to someone in sight or at hand; whereas if he had to look or wait for you, the chance would be lost. And to lose an opportunity, no matter how small, often means losing the introduction and access to great things.

*   *   *

135. I THINK the friars are mad to go around preaching on predestination and on the difficult articles of the faith. It is better not to have people think about things they can barely understand than to awaken doubt in their minds. For then, to quiet these doubts, they must resort to saying, "That is what our faith teaches, that is what we must believe."

*   *   *

136. IN FLORENCE, even a man who is a good citizen and not an enemy of liberty must be wary of getting very close to a regime such as this one of the Medici. For if he does, he will be suspected and disliked by the people; and that is to be avoided as much as possible because of the many consequences it can bring. But I also maintain that you should not, because of this risk, retire and lose all the benefits such intimacy with the regime could bring. As long as you do not gain a reputation for rapacity or offend important people, you will find that when the regime changes and the people have got rid of the cause that rendered

you odious, the other charges against you will be dropped, and
your bad favor will eventually wear away. You will not remain
in the state of ruin or disrepute you at first feared. Nevertheless,
these are weighty matters, and men can easily make mistakes on
them. Nor can it be denied that at best you will lose some of
that good reputation which is preserved by those who steered
clear of any involvement.

* * *

137. I SAY it to you again: masters have very little consideration
for their servants and will mistreat them terribly for the slightest
reason. And so those servants who act the same way toward their
masters are wise, so long as they do nothing contrary to faith
and honor.

* * *

138. IF A MAN knows he enjoys good fortune, he can undertake
things with greater confidence. But we should remember that
fortune not only varies from time to time, but may also vary
at the same time in different things. If you observe carefully,
you will sometimes see that men are fortunate in one sort of
thing and unfortunate in another. In my own case, up to this
day, February 3, 1523,[5] I have had very good fortune in many
things, but not in business nor in attaining those honors that I
have sought. Those I did not seek heaped themselves upon me,
but those I wanted seemed to move ever farther away.

* * *

139. MAN'S GREATEST enemy is himself. For nearly all of the
many evils, dangers, and worries he has to bear have their origin
in his excessive cupidity.

* * *

140. THE THINGS of this world do not stay fixed. In fact, they always progress along the road on which they should, according
to their nature, come to their end. But they move more slowly

5 The Florentine calendar begins its new year on March 25. This date is
therefore February 3, 1524, our style. During the republic G. was considered head of an anti-Soderini party. His position became delicate
enough for him to go into voluntary exile.

than we believe. We measure them by our lives, which are brief, and not according to their own time, which is long. But their movements are slower than ours—so slow, by their very nature, that although they move we do not notice it. And for that reason, the judgments we make concerning them are often wrong.

* * *

141. To DESIRE riches for no other reason than their enjoyment would be a sign of a base and deformed spirit. But life in this world being as corrupt as it is, anyone who wants a reputation is forced to seek wealth. For with wealth, those virtues shine and are esteemed which in a poor man are scarcely regarded and hardly known.

* * *

142. PERHAPS THOSE to whom a great opportunity presents itself once should not be called fortunate, for only a very prudent man will know how to take proper advantage of it. But without doubt, those to whom the same great opportunity presents itself twice are most fortunate indeed, for a man who did not know how to take advantage of it the second time would certainly be a fool. And thus, in the second case, everything is owed to fortune, whereas in the first, prudence also plays a part.

* * *

143. IN A REPUBLIC liberty is the servant of justice. It is not ordained for any purpose other than to prevent one man from being oppressed by another. Therefore, if we could be certain that in a government by one or by the few, justice would reign, we would have no cause to desire liberty very much. This is the reason that ancient wise men and philosophers did not praise free governments more than others but preferred those that best assured the maintenance of law and justice.

* * *

144. WHEN NEWS is brought from a doubtful source and seems probable and expected, I hesitate to believe it. For men easily

invent what seems expected or is credible. I listen more readily
if it is extraordinary or unexpected news, for men are far less
apt to invent or believe that which no one has in mind. I have
experienced this sort of thing many times.

*　　*　　*

145. How LUCKY astrologers are! Their art is a vain one, because of defects either in the art itself or in them. And yet they
gain more believers by predicting one thing that turns out true
than they lose by a hundred predictions that turn out false;
whereas, when other men are known to have told one lie,
people hesitate to believe anything they say, no matter how
true. This comes about because men have such a great desire to
know the future. Not having any other way, they readily
believe anyone who says he knows how to tell it, just as the in-
valid believes the doctor who promises him health.

*　　*　　*

146. PRAY TO GOD that you do not find yourself on the losing
side. For though you may be guiltless, you will nevertheless be
dicredited. Nor will it help to go about the streets and the
squares trying to justify yourself. Contrariwise, he who finds
himself among the winners will always receive praise, even if he
doesn't deserve it.

*　　*　　*

147. As EVERYONE knows, in private affairs it is an advantage to
be in possession, even though the legal right is not affected, and
even though judicial procedures for determining ownership of
property are well known and fixed. But it is an incomparably
greater advantage in matters that depend on the policy of the
state or on the will of those who rule. For, not having to fight
against immutable principles of reason or against established
decisions, you can easily use the thousands of accidents that
happen every day against anyone who seeks to remove you from
possession.

*　　*　　*

148. IF YOU want to be loved by your superiors, show respect

and reverence for them—and, in fact, rather too much than too little. For nothing offends a superior more than to think he is not receiving the respect and reverence he believes his due.

* * *

149. THE DECREE of the Syracusans, of which Livy makes mention, that even the daughters of tyrants must be killed, was indeed cruel, but it was not completely without reason. For when the tyrant is gone, those who gladly lived under him would do anything to create another, even if they had to make him out of wax. And since it is not easy to bestow reputation upon a new man, they will take advantage of anything that remains of the old one. Therefore, a city that has recently escaped from tyranny is never sure of its freedom unless it has extinguished the whole race and progeny of the tyrant. This applies absolutely to the males; as far as the females are concerned, I distinguish according to circumstances and according to the character of the women and of their cities.

* * *

150. I SAID earlier that states cannot be secured by cutting off heads, for this multiplies the number of enemies, as is said to be true of the Hydra. And yet there are many cases in which states must be held together with blood as buildings are with lime. There is no rule for distinguishing these opposite cases. They must be recognized by the prudence and discretion of him who faces them.

* * *

151. NOT EVERYONE is able to choose the station and the employment he desires. Rather, it is often necessary to accept what fate presents and to do what conforms to the station in which you were born. True merit, therefore, consists in conducting your own affairs well and in a seemly manner, just as, in a comedy, we do not have less praise for the actor who represents a servant well than for the actor who wears the robes of a king. In short, everyone can bring praise and honor to himself in his own station.

* * *

152. IN THIS world every man, no matter who he be, makes mistakes. They can cause more or less damage, depending upon the accidents and circumstances attendant upon them. Those men are fortunate who make mistakes that are unimportant or that cause small damage.

* * *

153. YOU ARE very fortunate if you can live in such a way that you neither offend people nor are offended by them. But if you are forced into a position in which you must either hurt or be hurt, be sure to make your move before someone else does. For in such circumstances whatever you do to escape harm is as justified as anything you do after you have been offended. True, you should distinguish each case carefully. You must not act out of groundless fear and then pretend you were forced to act first. Nor should you be so wicked or greedy as to allege this fear to justify the violence you do when, in fact, you have no reason for suspicion.

* * *

154. FOR ALL its greatness, the house of the Medici has a harder time keeping control of Florence than its ancestors, private citizens, had in acquiring it. The reason is that in those days the city had not yet tasted liberty and free institutions. Indeed, it was then always in the hands of a few. And he who controlled the state did not have the people as his enemy, since it mattered little to them whether the government was in the hands of these men or others. But the memory of popular government, which lasted from 1494 to 1512, is now so entrenched in the people that, except for those few who hope to have advantages under a despotism, the rest will be hostile to him who controls the state, for they will think he has taken what belongs to them.

* * *

155. LET NO MAN of Florence believe he can head the government if he is not of the line of Cosimo—indeed, even they need the support of the papacy to maintain themselves. No one else, no matter who he be, has strong enough roots or strong enough

following to even think of it, unless he be brought to the position by a popular government that needs a public head, as was the case with Piero Soderini. Thus, any man who aspires to such position, and is not of the Medici line, should side with the people.

* * *

156. THE DESIRES and decisions of the people are so unstable, so much more determined by chance than by reason, that it is senseless for any man to pin his hopes of achieving power on them. To guess what the people want is more a matter of luck than of wisdom.

* * *

157. IN FLORENCE, if you are the sort of man who cannot possibly hope to head the regime, you would be mad to get so involved with it that your whole lot depends on the regime's fate. For there is far more to lose than to gain. Nor should you ever run the risk of exile. For since we are not the heads of parties, like the Adorni and the Fregosi of Genoa,[6] no one is going to come forth with offers of hospitality. We would remain out in the cold, without reputation and without means, forced to beg for our lives. Abundant proof of this is offered by the case of Bernardo Rucellai,[7] if you remember him. The same reasoning should teach us to be politic and to get along with the head of the regime, so that he will have no cause to think we are enemies or to suspect us.

* * *

[6] The Fregosi and the Adorni held the office of doge many times in the turbulent period between 1339 and 1528. Their intense rivalry often caused the one family to go into exile while the other was in office, and to plot with other powers for their return. In G.'s time, Genoa passed under control of the Milanese and then of the French, with the Adorni governing in behalf of the former and the Fregosi plotting with Charles VIII, then with Louis XII, to gain control. When Andrea Doria finally freed the city from the French, who had gained control, the Fregosi and Adorni were so associated with turmoil and bloodshed that their very names were banned in Genoa.

[7] Bernardo Rucellai, counselor and relative of Lorenzo the Magnificent, continued to advise Piero de' Medici after Lorenzo's death in 1494. He fell out with Piero and soon found himself completely excluded from political power.

158. IF I could hope to effect them by myself, I would be quite willing to seek changes in governments I disliked. But when I remember that it requires getting involved with other men—and most of the time with mad and wicked men who know neither how to be silent nor how to act—there is nothing I abhor more than to think about such things.

* * *

159. THE TWO popes Julius and Clement had completely different characters.[8] The first had great, even limitless, courage: he was impulsive, impatient, open, and frank. The other had little courage, was perhaps even timid, very patient, moderate, and deceptive. And yet, men of such contrary natures could produce similar results and great achievements. For patience and impetuosity are both qualities with which a worthy prince can achieve great things. The one strikes swiftly and sweeps everything before it; the other uses time and occasion to weaken and conquer the enemy. In some matters, the one quality will be harmful and the other helpful. To be sure, any man who could combine them and use each at the proper time would be divine. But since such a combination is almost impossible, I believe that, *omnibus computatis,* greater things can be accomplished by patience and moderation than by impetuosity and boldness.

* * *

160. ALTHOUGH WE may act on the best advice, the future is so uncertain that the results are often contrary. Nevertheless, we must not surrender, like animals, a prey to fortune; rather we must follow reason, like men. The truly wise man should be more content to have acted on good advice though it yielded bad results than to have had good results from bad advice.

* * *

161. IF A man wants the favor of the people in Florence, he

8 Pope (1503–13) Julius II added new territories to the Papal State and succeeded to some degree in centralizing its administration. He was a hard fighter and a straightforward opponent, as much at home on a horse as on the papal throne. Pope Clement VII was the exact opposite in character (cf. n. 10 in series C).

must avoid a reputation for ambition; and he must never, even in trivial matters and in everyday life, try to seem superior, fancier, or more refined than others. For in a city completely founded on equality and full of envy, a man will of course be hated if the people think he does not want to be the equal of others or if he distinguishes his from the common mode of living.

* * *

162. IN MATTERS of economy, the main point is to cut off all superfluous expenditures. But true cleverness, it seems to me, consists in spending the same amount as others and getting more for your money; or, as is vulgarly said, to spend a quattrino and get five centsworth.

* * *

163. KEEP IN mind that although a man who earns money may spend something more than one who earns nothing, it is nevertheless madness to spend largely on the basis of your earnings, if you have not first accumulated some capital. For the chance to earn does not last forever, and if you do not make the most of it while it lasts, you will find, when it has passed, that you are as poor as you were before. What is more, you will have lost time and honor. For anyone who has had a good opportunity and not known how to use it will be considered a man of little sense. Keep this *ricordo* well in mind, for in my day I have seen many men go wrong here.

* * *

164. MY FATHER used to say, "A ducat in your purse does you more credit than ten you have spent." It is a maxim you should remember—not to become stingy or to fail to make honorable and reasonable expenditures, but as a brake against extravagance.

* * *

165. VERY RARELY are documents falsified at the start. Usually it is done later, when men have had time for wicked thoughts;

or else it is done when men notice, in their management of affairs, that a certain thing would be to their advantage, whereupon they try to make the instruments say what they would like them to have said. Therefore, when you have important documents drawn up, make it a habit to have them turned over to you immediately, and keep them at home in their authentic form.

* * *

166. IN FLORENCE, it is a great burden to have daughters, for it is very hard to marry them off well. To avoid mistakes in arranging a match, a father must measure very carefully his own position and the nature of actual circumstances. That will diminish his difficulty. But it will be increased if he thinks too highly of himself, or if he fails to see the way things are. I have often seen even wise fathers refuse alliances which they later wished for in vain. But neither should a man get so disgusted that, like Francesco Vettori, he gives his daughters away to the first man that asks for them. In short, it is a matter that—aside from the will of destiny—requires great prudence. I know much better what ought to be done than how to put it into practice when the occasion arises.

* * *

167. SURELY, SERVICES rendered to a people or to society at large are accounted less than those done to a particular person. Since they are done for the community, no one feels he has been personally served. Therefore, if you labor in behalf of a people or a community, you must not believe they will go to any trouble when you are in danger or need; nor should you believe that the memory of your services will cause them to forego their personal interests. Still, you must not think so ill of public services that you neglect an opportunity to render them. For such services gain you reputation and favor, and that is fruit enough for your troubles. Moreover, in some cases the memory will be useful to you; those affected by it may be moved to act in your favor. And if they are not moved as deeply as those you have benefited personally, they will at least act in

your favor in those cases where not too much effort is required. Moreover, there will be so many people who feel this mild sentiment, that the sum of their gratitude may be quite considerable.

* * *

168. THE FRUIT of good acts is not always visible. And so, very often, a man who is not satisfied to do good for its own sake does not do it at all, thinking he is wasting his time. But to think that, is no small mistake. For even if good acts bore no other visible fruit, they at least spread your good name and a good opinion of you. And that can be incredibly useful on many occasions and in many ways.

* * *

169. THE RULER of a land about to be attacked or beseiged must consider first of all any and all measures that will bring about delay. Even if he has no sure hope, he must welcome everything that steals time from the enemy, no matter how little. For often, another day, even another hour, will bring some accident that will save him.

* * *

170. IF YOU were to have a wise man judge what effects a particular event will have and then wrote down his judgment, you would find when you looked at it later that few of his predictions had come true; just as few as if, on New Year's Day, you looked at an astrologer's predictions for the previous year. The affairs of this world are simply too uncertain.

* * *

171. IN IMPORTANT matters, anyone who does not know the details well cannot form a sound judgment. Often one circumstance, though trivial, will change the whole case. But at times, I have seen a man who knows only the general facts of the case judge well, whereas the same person will judge poorly when he has heard the details. For men who do not have very good

minds and are not wholly free of passion will be easily confused
or change their minds as soon as they hear many details.

Supplement begun in April, 1528

172. WHEN YOU discuss the future, it is dangerous to make decisions by considering exhaustive possibilities; by saying, for instance, that either this or that must happen, and if this should
be the case I will do that, whereas if that should be the case,
I will do this. Often, a third or fourth possibility realizes itself,
beyond those you have presupposed. And then you will be non-
plussed because the ground on which your decision rested is
lacking.

* * *

173. NEVER REFUSE or hesitate to take steps against impending
dangers, especially in war, because you think they are too late.
Since things often take much longer than expected, because of
their very nature and because of the various obstacles they
encounter, it very often happens that the steps you omitted to
take, thinking they would be too late, would have been in time.
I have experienced this many times.

* * *

174. NEVER FAIL to do things that will bring you reputation,
just to please people and acquire friends. To the man who maintains or increases his reputation, friends and favors come of their
own accord. But a man who fails to do what he should will
lose respect; and he who has no reputation will also have no
friends and no popularity.

* * *

175. THE MORE you try to escape from one extreme by moving
towards the other, the more easily you will fall into the one
you fear, from not knowing how to stop on the middle ground.
Thus, the closer popular governments move toward license in
order to flee from tyranny, the more easily will they fall into it.

Alas, our compatriots in Florence do not understand this language.

* * *

176. WHENEVER WE want to do something about a law or some other thing that displeases us, it is an old custom in Florence to find a remedy by doing or ordaining the exact opposite of what we dislike. Afterwards, we find new defects, since all extremes are vicious, whereupon it becomes necessary to make other laws and other ordinances. That is one of the reasons we make new laws every day. We try to flee from the evils rather than find their true remedy.

* * *

177. WE OFTEN hear men say that if this had or had not been the case, that would or would not have happened. How wrong that reasoning is! For, if the truth could be known, the majority of times the results would have been the same, even if those factors we think might have changed things had been operative.

* * *

178. WHEN WICKED or ignorant men govern, it is not surprising that virtue and goodness are not esteemed. For the former hate them, and the latter do not know them.

* * *

179. PROVIDED A MAN does not disdain religion and good morals, is zealous for the welfare of his country, and does nothing to harm his neighbor, he is a perfectly good citizen. The excessive goodness of our friends at San Marco is often hypocrisy.[9] Even if it is not put on, it is, to be sure, not too much for a Christian but quite useless for the well being of the city.

* * *

180. THE MEDICI made a mistake in wanting to govern the state, in many ways, according to popular principles; for in-

* * *

[9] G. is referring to the monks in the Convent of Saint Mark's who, in this republican period, again played an active role in Florentine civil life.

stance, in making the candidacy lists large, giving everyone a share in civic business, and such things. A despotism could only be maintained in Florence with the fervent support of the few; but these methods neither made friends of the many nor partisans of the few. Popular government will be mistaken if it tries to govern according to the practices of a despotism—especially if it tries to exclude a part of the city. For popular government cannot be maintained without universal satisfaction. And since it cannot imitate a despotism in every respect, it is madness to imitate it in those respects that make it odious and not in those that make it strong.

*　*　*

181. "O INGENIA MAGIS ACRIA QUAM MATURA," said Petrarch, quite rightly, of the Florentines.[10] They are by nature lively and acute rather than grave and mature.

---

[10] The whole sentence reads: *O ingenia magis acuta quam solida, magis acria quam matura! Qui vos urit igniculas, quod virus inficit, quod calcar exagitat?* (Oh men of genius, more acute than solid, more sharp than mature! What fire burns you? What poison infects you? What spur pricks you?) In a letter to Boccaccio, dated 1363, in which Petrarch defends himself against his critics and their censure of some verses in his *Africa*.

Q^2

All of the thirteen *ricordi* contained in the first notebook (Q^1) are included, unchanged, in the second notebook (Q^2) which contains altogether twenty-nine *ricordi*. The numeration is the same, except that number twelve in the second notebook does not exist in the first, so that numbers twelve and thirteen of Q^1 are thirteen and fourteen of Q^2. All of the *ricordi* in Q^2 appear in B, but many are omitted in C, the final version.

1. ALTHOUGH LEISURE does not give birth to whims, it is indeed true that there can be no whims without leisure.

* * *

2. CITIZENS WHO seek reputation in their city are praiseworthy and useful, provided they seek it not by faction or usurpation but by striving to be considered good and prudent and by doing some good works for the public. Would to God that republics were full of such ambition!

* * *

3. IF A MAN is not really a good citizen, he will not long be thought one. Therefore, if he wants to give that impression, he must first strive to be good.

* * *

4. MEN ARE naturally inclined towards the good. Few, in fact, perhaps none, will do evil unless they expected some advantage or pleasure from it. True, the opportunities for drawing advantage from evil are many, so that men are easily deviated from their natural inclination. To keep them on it, the spur and the bridle were discovered, that is to say, rewards and punishments. When these are not used in a republic, you will very

rarely find good citizens. In Florence, we see it proved every day.

* * *

5. GREAT DEFECTS and failings are inherent in popular government. Nevertheless, wise and good citizens prefer it as a lesser evil.

* * *

6. WE MAY conclude that a wise man is also a good citizen. For given the way the world is, he would not be wise if he were not a good citizen.

* * *

7. THE SORT of generosity that pleases the public is very seldom found in a truly wise citizen. Therefore, a man who is more generous than wise is not to be commended.

* * *

8. THE PEOPLE love a just citizen. To the wise man they accord their reverence rather than love.

* * *

9. FEW WISE men are brave—not because bravery is the opposite of wisdom but because a wise man, knowing what the dangers are, will be afraid. But few have the additional strength to measure the danger reasonably. It is, therefore, a failing in a wise man not to be brave. In fact, a man who considers dangers to be greater than they really are, is not completely wise.

* * *

10. ONLY WISE men are brave. Others are either temerarious or foolhardy. Thus, we can say that every brave man is wise but not that every wise man is brave.

* * *

11. OH, GOD! how many more reasons there are to believe our republic will soon fail, than to think it will last a long time.

* * *

12. RULES ARE found written in books; exceptional cases are written in your discretion.

*   *   *

13. A MAN who has good sense can make great use of one who has many talents. And much more so than the other way around.

*   *   *

14. THE EQUALITY of men under a popular government is by no means contradicted if one citizen enjoys greater reputation than another, provided it proceed from the love and reverence of all, and can be withheld by the people at their pleasure. Indeed, without such supports, republics can hardly last. It would be a good thing for our city if the fools in Florence understood this well.

*   *   *

15. HE WHO must command others should not be too fastidious or scrupulous in giving orders. I do not say he must be without these qualities altogether; but too much is harmful to him.

*   *   *

16. IT IS very wise to manage your affairs secretely. But it is even more praiseworthy and more advantageous if you try as hard as you can not to appear secretive. For many men will become indignant when they see that you refuse to confide in them.

*   *   *

17. I WANT to see three things before I die: a well ordered republic in our city, Italy liberated from all the barbarians, and the world delivered from the tyranny of these wicked priests.

*   *   *

18. UNLESS YOUR safety is completely guaranteed by treaty or by such great strength that no matter what happens, you have nothing to fear, you are mad to stay neutral when others are

at war. For you do not satisfy the vanquished, and you remain prey to the victor. If you are not convinced by reason, look at the example of our city and what happened to it by remaining neutral in the war that Pope Julius and the Catholic King waged against Louis, king of France.

*   *   *

19. MEN ARE very false. Therefore, the best assurance against being hurt by someone must be founded in his inability and not in his unwillingness to hurt you.

*   *   *

20. THERE IS far greater pleasure in controlling lewd desires than in gratifying them. The latter is brief and of the body; the former—once our appetite has somewhat subsided—is long lasting and of the mind and conscience.

*   *   *

21. HONOR AND reputation are more to be desired than riches. But since nowadays a reputation can hardly be maintained without riches, virtuous men must seek them. But they must do so only to the extent and in such manner that suffices to have the effect of maintaining a reputation and authority.

*   *   *

22. OUR PEOPLE of Florence are poor and want very much to be rich. And for that reason they are unable to preserve the freedom of the city. For this appetite makes men pursue their personal advantage without respect or consideration for the public honor and glory.

*   *   *

23. THE MORTAR that holds together the rule of tyrants is the blood of citizens. Therefore, everyone should see to it that such edifices are not constructed in his city.

*   *   *

24. YOUNG MEN should realize that experience teaches a great

deal—and more to large minds than to small. Anyone who thinks about it will easily see the reason.

* * *

25. IF THE citizens of a republic are ruled by a government which—despite some defects—is tolerable, they should never try to change it for a better one, for it will nearly always get worse. The reason is that he who makes the change will not have the power to fashion the new government precisely according to his designs and thoughts.

* * *

26. THE MAJORITY of crimes committed by the powerful men in cities arises from suspicion. Therefore, when a man has become leader he must be treated with as much care as possible; nor ought anyone to move against him unless he is certain of winning.

* * *

27. DO NOT reveal your secrets to anyone unless forced by necessity, for you become the slave of those who know them. Furthermore, their being known may cause you harm. And even when necessity forces you to tell them, you should do so as late as possible. For when men have lots of time, they will think a thousand and one evil thoughts.

* * *

28. TO LET go occasionally, or, to put it better, to give vent to ones feelings of pleasure or anger, is a very comforting thing, but it is harmful. And therefore it is very wise not to do it; but it is very hard.

* * *

29. AMONG THE POOR, malevolence may be caused by some accident; in the rich, it is there only by nature. And therefore it is far more reprehensible in the rich than in the poor.

Tables of Correspondence

TABLE OF RICORDI CORRESPONDING TO SERIES C

C	Q²	B	C	Q²	B	C	Q²	B
1		—	36		87	70		61
2		24	37		47	71		140
3		—	38		154	72		34
4		69, 137	39		66	73		—
5		39, 40	40		74	74		—
6	12	35, 121	41	15	12, 8₅, 119, 120, 150	75		—
7	} 88		42		—	76		114
8	}		43		118	77		51
9		100	44	3	2	78		117
10		71	45		164	79		76
11		43	46		38	80		142
12		—	47		91	81		—
13		78	48		95	82		25
14		44	49		—	83		75
15		59	50		54	84		99
16		60	51		53	85		138
17		57	52		126	86		130
18		79	53		127	87		73
19		158	54		169	88		48
20		55	55		56	89		144
21		180	56		162	90		104
22		177	57		145	91		107
23		96	58		—	92		—
24		42	59		—	93		94
25		41	60		115	94		134
26		86	61		77	95		89
27	19	33	62		—	96	9, 10	90
28		124	63		63	97		30
29		131	64		—	98		
30		—	65		—	99		} 82, 83
31		52	66		106	100		
32	2	1	67		122	101		
33		65	68	18	15, 16	102		—
34		103	69		116	103		81
35		—				104		45, 46

C	Q²	B	C	Q²	B	C	Q²	B
105		—	144		129	183		—
106		166	145		98	184	27, 28	49, 50
107		—	146		—	185		—
108		152	147		—	186	16	13
109		143	148		—	187		—
110		—	149		—	188		175, 176
111		—	150		—	189		—
112		—	151		—	190		—
113		68	152		—	191		—
114		—	153		—	192		—
115		—	154		—	193		—
116		—	155		171	194		—
117		—	156		—	195		—
118		105	157		—	196		—
119		165	158		168	197		—
120	26	22	159		—	198		—
121		156	160		—	199		—
122		—	161		—	200		—
123		—	162		173	201		—
124		—	163		36	202		—
125		—	164		—	203		113
126		—	165		133	204		—
127		28	166		—	205		—
128		97	167		—	206		—
129		128	168		—	207		—
130		—	169		—	208		—
131		84	170		—	209		67
132		—	171		—	210		—
133		102	172		92, 93	211		—
134	4	3	173		72	212		—
135		4	174 }		37	213		—
136		—	175 }			214		—
137		—	176		146	215		62
138		80	177		—	216		151
139		—	178		—	217		174
140		123	179		—	218		—
141		—	180		—	219		—
142		—	181		—	220		108
143		—	182		172	221		—

TABLE OF RICORDI CORRESPONDING TO SERIES B

B	C	Q^2
motto	—	1
1	32	2
2	44	3
3	134	4
4	135	—
5	—	5
6	—	6
7	—	7
8	—	8
9	—	11
10	—	13
11	—	14
12	41	15
13	186	16
14	—	17
15 / 16	} 68	18
17	—	20
18	—	21
19	—	22
20	—	23
21	—	25
22	120	26
23	—	29
24	2	
25	82	
26	—	
27	—	
28	127	
29	—	
30	97	
31	—	
32	—	
33	27	19
34	72	
35	6	12
36	163	
37	174, 175	
38	46	
39 / 40	} 5	
41	25	
42	24	

B	C	Q^2
43	11	
44	14	
45 / 46	} 104	
47	37	
48	88	
49 / 50	} 184	} 27 / 28
51	77	
52	31	
53	51	
54	50	
55	20	
56	55	
57	17	
58	—	
59	15	
60	16	
61	70	
62	215	
63	63	
64	—	
65	33	
66	39	
67	209	
68	113	
69	4	
70	—	24
71	10	
72	173	
73	87	
74	40	
75	83	
76	79	
77	61	
78	13	
79	18	
80	138	
81	103	
82 / 83	} 98, 99 / 100, 101 }	
84	131	
85	41	15

B	C	Q^2
86	26	
87	36	
88	7, 8	
89	95	
90	96	9, 10
91	47	
92 / 93	} 172	
94	93	
95	48	
96	23	
97	128	
98	145	
99	84	
100	9	
101	—	
102	133	
103	34	
104	90	
105	118	
106	66	
107	91	
108	220	
109	—	
110	—	
111	—	
112	—	
113	203	
114	76	
115	60	
116	69	
117	78	
118	43	
119 / 120	} 41	15
121	6	12
122	67	
123	140	
124	28	
125	—	
126	52	
127	53	
128	129	

B	C	Q^2	B	C	Q^2	B	C	Q^2
129	144		147	—		165	119	
130	86		148	—		166	106	
131	29		149	—		167	—	
132	—		150	41	15	168	158	
133	165		151	216		169	54	
134	94		152	108		170	—	
135	—		153	—		171	155	
136	—		154	38		172	182	
137	4		155	—		173	162	
138	85		156	121		174	217	
139	—		157	—		175	} 188	
140	71		158	19		176		
141	—		159	—		177	22	
142	80		160	—		178	—	
143	109		161	—		179	—	
144	89		162	56		180	21	
145	57		163	—		181	—	
146	176		164	45				

TABLE OF RICORDI CORRESPONDING TO SERIES Q^2

Q^2	B	C	Q^2	B	C	Q^2	B	C
1	motto	—	11	9	—	20	17	—
2	1	32	12	35, 121	6	21	18	—
3	2	44	13	10	—	22	19	—
4	3	134	14	11	—	23	20	—
5	5	—	15	} 12, 85, 119, 120, 150	} 41	24	70	—
6	6	—				25	21	—
7	7	—	16	13	186	26	22	120
8	8	—	17	14	—	27	49	} 184
9	} 90	} 96	18	15-16	68	28	50	
10			19	33	27	29	23	—

Pennsylvania Paperbacks

Pennsylvania Paperbacks continued